A "Scottsboro" Case in Mississippi

A "Scottsboro" Case in Mississippi

The Supreme Court and *Brown* v. *Mississippi*

By
Richard C. Cortner

UNIVERSITY PRESS OF MISSISSIPPI
Jackson and London

MANUFACTURED IN THE UNITED STATES OF AMERICA
Print-on-Demand Edition
The paper in this book meets the guidelines for permanence and durability
of the Committee on Production Guidelines for Book Longevity of the
Council on Library Resources.

Library of Congress Cataloging-in-Publication Data

Cortner, Richard C.
  A "Scottsboro" case in Mississippi.

  Bibliography: p.
  Includes index.
  1. Brown, Ed—Trials, litigation, etc.   2. Trials
(Murder)—Mississippi—DeKalb.   3. Right to counsel—
United States.   4. Confession (Law)—United States.
I. Title.
KF224.B76C67 1986   345.73'02523   85-20174
ISBN 087805-284-4   347.3052523

Contents

*This book is dedicated to the
memories of two Mississippians of
uncommon courage*

John A. Clark, of DeKalb,
and
Earl Leroy Brewer, of Jackson

Preface

Ratified in 1868 in the wake of the Civil War, the Fourteenth Amendment to the United States Constitution profoundly altered the nature of the federal system. As a consequence of decisions of the United States Supreme Court interpreting the Due Process Clause of the Fourteenth Amendment, most of the rights guaranteed in the Bill of Rights as limitations originally upon the powers of the national government have been held by the Court to apply to exercises of power by state and local governments as well. This "nationalization" of the Bill of Rights not only fundamentally changed the nature of the federal system under the Constitution, but it also made the guarantees of fundamental liberties in the Bill of Rights more salient to the average citizen than ever before.[1]

For many years after the ratification of the Fourteenth Amendment, however, the Supreme Court narrowly construed the Due Process Clause of the amendment with regard to the protection of civil liberties, and, indeed, in several cases the Court adamantly rejected the idea that the Due Process Clause might be interpreted to protect, against state action, the rights in the Bill of Rights.[2] As late as the 1920s, therefore, the Due Process Clause had not been interpreted to impose upon the powers of the states any significant restrictions regarding civil liberties.[3]

During the 1920s, however, the Supreme Court significantly changed its construction of the Due Process Clause as a vehicle by which civil liberties could be protected against state action. In *Gitlow* v. *New York,* decided in 1925, the Court declared that for "present purposes we may and do assume that freedom of speech and of the press—which are protected by the 1st Amendment from abridgment by Congress—are among the fundamental personal rights and 'liberties' protected by the due process clause of the 14th Amendment from impairment by the states."[4] And what had been stated only as an assumption in the *Gitlow* case became a reality in the decisions of the Court by 1931, when the Court explicitly held freedom of speech and freedom of the press to be protected against state interference by the Due Process Clause of the Fourteenth Amendment.[5] Indeed, by 1947 the Court had nationalized all of the rights in the First Amendment of the Bill of Rights by holding that the Due Process Clause imposed them upon the states.[6]

In addition to the breakthrough regarding the nationalization of First Amendment rights in the *Gitlow* case, the 1920s also witnessed a similar breakthrough in the field of criminal procedure. Until the 1920s, the Supreme Court had held that the Due Process Clause merely required the states in the conduct of criminal trials to provide adequate notice of the charges against a criminal defendant and a fair trial according to the traditional modes of proceeding under the common law. And the Court had also demonstrated considerable reluctance to look behind the mere forms of state criminal proceedings to determine whether the states were in fact affording criminal defendants fair trials.[7]

However, in *Moore* v. *Dempsey*, decided in 1923, the Court held that for the states to afford defendants the mere form of a fair trial was no longer sufficient and that the Due Process Clause required a fair trial in fact as well as form. Condemning the mob domination of a trial in Arkansas in which six blacks had been sentenced to death, Justice Oliver Wendell Holmes, Jr., eloquently declared the Court's shift in due process philosophy regarding state criminal procedure. If "the case is," Holmes said, "that the whole proceeding [in a state criminal trial] is a mask,—that counsel, jury, and judge were swept to the fatal end by an irresistible wave of public passion, and that the state courts failed to correct the wrong,—neither perfection in the machinery for correction nor the possibility that the trial court and counsel saw no other way of avoiding an immediate outbreak of the mob can prevent this court from securing to the . . . [state criminal defendants] their constitutional rights."[8]

The shift in the Court's approach to the interpretation of the Due Process Clause in *Moore* v. *Dempsey* was as important in the field of criminal procedure as the shift in the *Gitlow* case was in relation to First Amendment freedoms. For after the decision in *Moore* v. *Dempsey*, the Court insisted that the states must afford criminal defendants fair trials in fact as well as form, and the Court began to scrutinize state criminal cases more critically under the Due Process Clause. The result was that in subsequent cases involving the trials of state criminal defendants, the Court began to define what a fair trial under the Due Process Clause meant, and in the process the Court held that the right to a fair trial required the states to afford to defendants rights that were at least similar to the criminal-procedure guarantees contained in the Bill of Rights.

By the 1930s, consequently, the Supreme Court had laid the basis for a profound change in the protection of civil liberties under the Constitution, and under the fair-trial rule of *Moore* v. *Dempsey* it had paved the way for the imposition of more rigorous federal constitutional standards in state criminal proceedings. The Depression decade therefore became a watershed in the Court's approach to criminal procedure under the Due Process Clause, since in two landmark cases the Court further expanded the federal constitutional standards applicable in state criminal proceedings and laid the groundwork for the subsequent development of criminal-procedure protections under the Due Process Clause.

These two cases were *Powell* v. *Alabama*, decided in 1932,[9] and *Brown* v. *Mississippi*, decided in 1936.[10] *Powell* v. *Alabama*, which became an international cause célèbre during the 1930s, was popularly known as the Scottsboro case, since it involved nine indigent black youths who were charged with the capital crime of rape, and who were indicted, tried, convicted, and, except for one, sentenced to death at Scottsboro, Alabama, in 1931. In reversing these convictions in the *Powell* case in 1932, the Supreme Court held that the right to a fair trial mandated by the Due Process Clause required the appointment of counsel for indigent defendants in capital cases, and if the lack of representation by counsel would result in an unfair trial to an indigent defendant in a non-capital case, counsel must be appointed in non-capital cases as well.[11] Because there had been no adequate representation by counsel for the Scottsboro youths at their trials, the Court reversed their convictions in *Powell* v. *Alabama*. And in doing so, the Court began the expansion of the constitutional right to counsel that would culminate with decisions in the 1960s holding that indigent defendants had the right to appointed counsel in any criminal proceeding involving potential loss of liberty for the defendant.[12]

The Alabama Scottsboro litigation received extensive contemporary national and even international publicity, and it has since been the subject of much scholarly analysis.[13] The Supreme Court's second path-breaking decision in the field of criminal procedure during the 1930s—the decision in *Brown* v. *Mississippi* in 1936—largely escaped, on the other hand, any contemporary national publicity, and until now has not been the subject of scholarly analysis. Ironically, however, the *Brown* case was commonly referred to in Mississippi at the time as the "Mississippi Scottsboro Case" because of its similarity to the Scottsboro, Alabama, litigation. And despite the lack of contemporaneous attention that it received, *Brown* v. *Mississippi* was equal in importance as a landmark in the constitutional law of criminal procedure to the decision in *Powell* v. *Alabama*.[14]

For in the *Brown* case, the Supreme Court for the first time reversed a state criminal conviction on the ground that the conviction was based upon confessions coerced from the defendants and thus applied the Constitution to police interrogations of criminal suspects. *Brown* v. *Mississippi* as a consequence became a landmark case in the jurisprudence of the Supreme Court, since in that case the Court took the first step down the path of constitutional development that would lead thirty years later to the controversial decision in *Miranda* v. *Arizona*, a decision requiring the police to warn suspects of their right to silence and right to counsel before in-custody

interrogation could occur.[15] Because of the pivotal importance
of the decision in *Brown* v. *Mississippi* to the modern constitutional law of criminal procedure, it is the purpose of this book
to analyze the litigation that resulted in the *Brown* decision and
to explore the circumstances that produced the case and that
ultimately brought it to the Supreme Court for decision.

This analysis of the *Brown* case not only reveals a rather
dramatic story of constitutional litigation, but also unfortunately must deal with the human tragedy that characterized
so much of the case. *Brown* v. *Mississippi* began with tragedy:
It was a murder case involving a white planter, Raymond
Stuart, who was brutally beaten to death in his rural home in
Kemper County, Mississippi, in the spring of 1934. The tragedy and the brutality did not end with Stuart's murder, however. Three black tenant farmers—Ed Brown, Henry Shields,
and Arthur (Yank) Ellington—were arrested and tortured until
they confessed to the murder of Stuart. And amid threats of
mob violence and lynching, Brown, Shields, and Ellington
were hastily indicted, tried before an all-white jury, convicted,
and sentenced to death by hanging, the coerced confessions
being the principal evidence against them. Only one week
separated the discovery of Raymond Stuart's body and the
imposition of death sentences upon the three black defendants.

Given the racial prejudice that prevailed in Mississippi
during the 1930s, by all odds the *Brown* case would ordinarily
have ended with the hanging of Brown, Shields, and Ellington
in the yard of the Kemper County jail at DeKalb in the spring
of 1934. However, one of the attorneys appointed by the
Mississippi trial court to defend the three blacks—John A.
Clark of DeKalb—was conscience-stricken by the treatment to
which the blacks had been subjected, and he resolved to appeal
their convictions to the Mississippi Supreme Court. A state
senator with what appeared to be a promising political future,
John Clark nevertheless lost the appeal in the state supreme
court. His defense of Brown, Shields, and Ellington not only
destroyed his political career but the pressure of the case also
caused him to suffer a mental and physical collapse from which
he never recovered. Earl Leroy Brewer, a former governor of

Mississippi, was then persuaded to enter the case as defense counsel, and it was he who conducted the successful appeal to the U.S. Supreme Court.

The litigation in *Brown* v. *Mississippi* involved more than the individual courage of John Clark and Earl Brewer. It also revealed the role that interest groups can play in the judicial process. Because Brown, Shields, and Ellington were indigent tenant farmers, a coordinated effort to finance the litigation on their behalf was crucial to a successful appeal to the U.S. Supreme Court, and interest-group support for their cause became vital to their defense. Such support finally appeared when the *Brown* case attracted the attention and financial backing of three groups interested in the promotion of racial justice—the National Association for the Advancement of Colored People (NAACP), the Commission on Interracial Cooperation (CIC), and the Association of Southern Women for the Prevention of Lynching (ASWPL). At that point *Brown* v. *Mississippi* became an example of intergroup cooperation in the judicial process.

The *Brown* case was appealed to the U.S. Supreme Court at a crucial time as far as doctrinal development under the Due Process Clause of the Fourteenth Amendment was concerned, since the Court was only in the early stages of scrutinizing state criminal trials more closely under the Due Process Clause and insisting that such trials be procedurally fair in fact as well as form. Chief Justice Charles Evans Hughes's opinion for a unanimous Court in the *Brown* case declared that the use of coerced confessions to secure criminal convictions was a denial of due process in the most fundamental sense. Although the states had broad latitude in the regulation of procedures in criminal trials, Chief Justice Hughes eloquently declared in his *Brown* opinion, they could not adopt "trial by ordeal. The rack and the torture chamber may not be substituted for the witness stand."[16] The *Brown* case thus involves a compelling story of the process of constitutional litigation but illuminates as well the role of the Supreme Court as a vehicle of constitutional change in the United States.

During the course of my research on *Brown* v. *Mississippi*, I was extended much-welcomed courtesy and cooperation by the staffs of four libraries—the University of Arizona Library; the Manuscript Division of the Library of Congress; the Seeley G. Mudd Library, at Princeton University; and the Atlanta University Center–Woodruff Library in Atlanta, Georgia. To the staffs of these libraries, I express my deepest appreciation for their valuable help. My work on the *Brown* litigation was also aided substantially by Claudia Brewer Strite. As the only surviving daughter of former governor Earl Leroy Brewer of Mississippi, Mrs. Strite responded generously to my questions regarding her father and his role in the litigation and also furnished me with his unpublished biography, a work that significantly furthered my research. I express my gratitude to Mrs. Strite for her kind help as well as her enthusiastic encouragement as my work on the *Brown* case progressed.

The story that follows presents the anatomy of a constitutional law case that proved to be a critical juncture in American constitutional development. But it is also a story revealing human nature at its best and at its worst, with courage, decency, and self-sacrifice contrasting graphically with bigotry, brutality, and indifference. In the final analysis, the story of *Brown* v. *Mississippi* demonstrates the fragility of the barriers that separate us from human savagery, and the importance of maintaining those barriers constitutional and otherwise, in preserving a civilized society.

1. For an analysis of the nationalization of the Bill of Rights, see Richard C. Cortner, *The Supreme Court and the Second Bill of Rights* (Madison: University of Wisconsin Press, 1981).

2. See Hurtado v. California, 110 U.S. 516 (1884); Spies v. Illinois, 123 U.S. 131 (1887); Maxwell v. Dow, 176 U.S. 581 (1900); Brown v. New Jersey, 175 U.S. 172 (1899); Prudential Insurance Co. v. Cheek, 259 U.S. 530 (1922).

3. In Chicago, Burlington & Quincy Railroad Co. v. Chicago, 166 U.S. 226 (1897), the Court did hold, however, that the Due Process Clause prohibited the states from taking private property for a public purpose without just compensation, a right also protected by the Fifth Amendment of the Bill of Rights.

4. Gitlow v. New York, 268 U.S. 652, 665–66 (1925).

5. Near v. Minnesota, 283 U.S. 697 (1931); Stromberg v. California, 283 U.S. 359 (1931).

6. See Cortner, *Supreme Court and Second Bill of Rights,* pp. 63–123.

7. See Frank v. Mangum, 237 U.S. 309 (1915).

8. Moore v. Dempsey, 261 U.S. 86, 91 (1923).

9. Powell v. Alabama, 287 U.S. 56 (1932).

10. Brown v. Mississippi, 297 U.S. 278 (1936).

11. This was, at least, ultimately the received understanding of the *Powell* decision; see Betts v. Brady, 316 U.S. 455 (1942).

12. Gideon v. Wainwright, 372 U.S. 335 (1963); Argersinger v. Hamlin, 407 U.S. 25 (1972).

13. See Dan T. Carter, *Scottsboro: A Tragedy of the American South,* rev. ed. (Baton Rouge: Louisiana State University Press, 1979), for an excellent analysis of the Scottsboro litigation.

14. As Loren Miller noted in his book *The Petitioners* (New York: Pantheon Books, 1966), pp. 277–78, *Brown* v. *Mississippi* was "as classic in the sphere of confessions as the first Scottsboro case was in the right to counsel and time for preparation of a defense."

15. Miranda v. Arizona, 387 U.S. 436 (1966).

16. Brown v. Mississippi, 297 U.S. 278, 285–86 (1936).

A "Scottsboro" Case in Mississippi

I

A Murder In Bloody Kemper

In March 1934, President Franklin D. Roosevelt had only a year previously assured the nation that "the only thing we have to fear is fear itself" in the face of the economic devastation of the Depression. Despite the inauguration of the New Deal, the hand of the Depression still lay very heavily upon the nation, and especially was this so in the agricultural South, where economic survival for sharecroppers and tenant farmers was difficult enough in normal times. After a tour of the South in the mid-1930s, Secretary of Agriculture Henry Wallace was deeply shocked by what he had seen, and reported that he had "never seen among the peasantry of Europe poverty so abject as that which exists . . . in the great cotton States from Arkansas on to the East Coast. . . . I am tempted to say that one third of the farmers of the United States live under conditions which are so much worse than the peasantry of Europe that the city people of the United States should be thoroughly ashamed."[1]

The depressed economic conditions also exacerbated relations between blacks and whites in the South, with the result that the number of lynchings of blacks, which had declined from 1900 to 1930, increased again in the 1930s.[2] In some instances, lynchings were avoided when lynch mobs were assured by officials and the press that "the law should take its course," and rapid indictments and trials were arranged for black defendants. These defendants were usually inadequately represented by counsel, and were quickly sentenced to death, after verdicts of guilty from all-white juries. This "legal lynching" allowed the forms of the law to be observed, and permitted officials and the press to congratulate the community for its devotion to due process of law, while the end sought by the lynch mob was also achieved. Just such a procedure had been followed in the notorious Scottsboro case in Alabama in 1931— nine black youths charged with the capital crime of rape were indicted, tried, and convicted, and eight of them were sentenced to death within just over two weeks of the alleged crime.[3]

The defense of the Scottsboro defendants would become a cause célèbre during the 1930s, but largely overlooked was the fact that in Kemper County, Mississippi, approximately 150 miles southwest of Scottsboro, Alabama, a carbon copy of the Scottsboro proceedings occurred in the spring of 1934. Kemper County is located in the east-central part of Mississippi, bordering the state of Alabama on the east. During the 1930s, Kemper County was a predominately rural, cotton-farming area dotted with small communities. The county seat was the town of DeKalb, with a population in 1930 of 888, while the population of Kemper County as a whole was 21,881. The urban center nearest to Kemper County was the city of Meridian, located some thirty miles south of DeKalb in Lauderdale County. In a state in which the lynching of blacks for alleged crimes was not uncommon, Kemper County whites had demonstrated an even greater propensity to resort to the lynching of blacks than their fellow Mississippians. The number of lynchings in Kemper County was twice the rate that it was in the rest of the state. For this reason, Kemper County had come to be known by the 1930s as "Bloody Kemper."[4]

Indeed, on 10 September 1930, Kemper County achieved the dubious distinction of having a double lynching. "Pig" Lockett and Holly White, two Kemper County blacks, were accused of robbing a white couple and threatening their lives. Lockett and White were lodged in the county jail in DeKalb, but were taken from sheriff's deputies as they were being transported to Scooba, a small community east of DeKalb, for a preliminary hearing. The lynch mob tied ropes to two small trees, bending them over and securing the ends of the ropes around the necks of Lockett and White. The trees were then allowed to spring into an upright position, thus tightening the ropes around the necks of the two blacks. This process was repeated several times, as the mob sought to force confessions from the two men. One finally strangled to death without admitting his guilt, while the other allegedly gasped out a confession before he too was hanged. An observer reported that as the trees were allowed to spring into an upright position, the blacks would be jerked up at the ends of the ropes "like a kitten."[5]

The leaders of this lynch mob were reported to be leaders in the Scooba community and were "prominently identified with the local church, school and other community activities." One of the members of the mob, a local planter who was active in the local church, purchased two cheap coffins for Lockett and White in Scooba after having participated in their lynching. It would be sacrilegious, he indicated, not to give the victims of the mob "a decent burial."[6]

On Friday, 30 March 1934, in the Giles community six miles east of Scooba, Raymond Stuart, a sixty-year-old white planter, was found at his home dying of wounds that appeared to have been inflicted with an ax. Stuart's slaying shocked and stunned not only the residents of Giles, Scooba, and DeKalb in Kemper County, but also the residents of Meridian, where Stuart had frequently visited his brother, Burt Stuart, a Meridian architect and former city engineer. "Raymond Stuart was well known and highly esteemed here," the Meridian *Star* noted in its front-page coverage of his murder. "He was of a quiet, unassuming disposition, winning friends easily and often entertained Meridian friends at his home where he lived alone and was a great lover of the outdoors. News of his tragic death was received with a great shock by his many friends here as well as throughout the section where he had so long resided."[7]

Raymond Stuart's neighbors, the *Star* reported, had noticed his absence from his regular schedule of duties and had checked on him at his home. Although Stuart was still alive when found, and a physician was summoned, he almost immediately succumbed to his wounds. Scooba city marshal T. H. Nicholson stated to the press that robbery was the apparent motive for the murder, while T. D. Harbour, the chief detective of the Meridian police department, who also was summoned to the scene of the murder, reported that there had been an attempt to burn Stuart's house after he had been attacked. A lamp had been smashed, and Stuart's right shoulder sleeve and part of his face had been slightly burned, but the fire had failed to spread. Chief detective Harbour examined the murder scene for fingerprints and reportedly obtained some good samples, and he stated that in his opinion "the murder had been committed with the sharp point of a pick or some such instrument, the skull being penetrated." Indeed, the Meridian *Star* reported, "Mr. Stuart's head was beaten almost to a pulp."[8]

As the news of Raymond Stuart's murder spread in Kemper County, mob action appeared to be threatening as two hundred persons gathered outside Stuart's home. Kemper County sheriff J. D. Adcock and several deputies rushed to the scene, and bloodhounds were used in an attempt to track the perpetrators of the crime, but the large crowd gathered at the murder scene had obliterated any trail that the bloodhounds might have been able to follow. Sheriff Adcock nevertheless arrested Ed Brown, a thirty-year-old black tenant on Stuart's farm, and held him in the Kemper County jail in DeKalb in connection with the murder.[9]

On the day after the arrest of Ed Brown, Henry Shields, a twenty-seven-year-old black who lived a half mile from Raymond Stuart's house, was arrested by Meridian police and Kemper County deputies in Meridian. Apparently fearing for the safety of Brown and Shields if they continued to be confined in the Kemper County jail in DeKalb, Sheriff Adcock ordered the prisoners to be transferred to the Lauderdale County jail in Meridian.[10]

Ed Brown and Henry Shields, the Meridian *Star* reported, were interrogated in the Lauderdale County jail by Meridian chief of police B. B. Hyde, Meridian chief of detectives T. D. Harbour, Scooba city marshal T. H. Nicholson, and Kemper County deputy sheriff Cliff M. Dial, and both suspects ultimately confessed to their participation in the murder of Raymond Stuart. According to press reports of the confessions, the motive for the murder of Stuart had been robbery, and he had been attacked as he slept, being struck first "with a big sweetgum stick" and subsequently beaten on the head with a "foot adz, a sharp edged tool for wood working, which after it had been brutally wielded had been thrown into a well near the rear porch of the Stuart home and which has not yet been recovered."[11]

"When confronted with a bloodstained jumper and pair of overalls that were said to have been found with a search of his home [and] on which was found some strands of hair similar in color to that of the murdered planter," the Meridian *Star* reported, "the negro Shields was said to have broken down and made a statement that implicated Ed Brown, Stuart plantation tenant, taken into custody shortly after Mr. Stuart had been found in a dying condition." "Brown," the *Star* continued, "who is also being held in the Lauderdale county jail, was said to have been next questioned, with the result that he also is alleged to have admitted his part in the brutal slaying, the purported statements of each being corroborative."[12]

On 3 April, the day following this report of the confessions of Ed Brown and Henry Shields, the arrest of yet another suspect in the murder of Raymond Stuart was reported in the press. Arthur Ellington, a twenty-year-old black who lived near the Stuart farm, was reported to have been arrested April 2 in Kemper County by Deputy Sheriff Cliff Dial, "who took him in custody and hurried him by devious routes to Meridian." "Ellington," the Meridian *Star* reported, "according to Deputy Dial, made practically the same statement that was said to have been made by the other two blacks."[13]

The reports of the arrests of Ed Brown, Henry Shields, and Arthur Ellington, along with their purported confessions detailing the brutality with which Raymond Stuart had been murdered, apparently stirred deep feelings both in Kemper

County and in Meridian. With all three of the suspects lodged in the Lauderdale County jail in Meridian, there were persistent reports that a mob would attack the jail and attempt to lynch the prisoners, prompting Sheriff B. M. Stephens to take precautionary measures. "The jail from early nightfall [on 2 April]," the Meridian *Star* thus reported, "was filled with deputies, others were stationed at vantage points in the vicinity of the jail block, while the prison itself bristled with machine guns, sawed-off shotguns, tear gas bombs and other emergency equipment. . . ." Sheriff Stephens also inquired regarding the mobilization of the local National Guard unit if necessary, but in the event, no attempt was made to mob the jail and lynch Brown, Shields, and Ellington.[14]

In what was an obvious attempt by officials to reduce the possibility of a lynching, it was announced to the press that Brown, Shields, and Ellington would be indicted and tried for murder in very short order. The suspects, the Meridian *Star* thus reported, were to be given "a speedy trial at the present term of the Kemper county circuit court. Presiding Judge J. I. Sturdivant, it is believed, will recall the Kemper county grand jury and should indictments be brought, the trials of the accused would follow without any more delay than is absolutely necessary under the procedure required by law." "A speedy trial for the suspected blacks would go a long way," the *Star* said, "toward removing any apprehension of attempted violence on the part of allegedly enraged citizens of Kemper, in the expressed opinion of officials and others."[15]

Brown, Shields, and Ellington, it was also reported, repeated their confessions on 2 April to the Kemper County sheriff, J. D. Adcock, Lauderdale County sheriff B. M. Stephens, and others at the jail in Meridian. "After the Kemper county planter had been beaten to near death, the weapons being an axe, cold chisel and the final death-dealing foot adz," the Meridian *Star* reported, "the purported statements of the suspects were to the effect that after the almost lifeless man had been thrown into the cotton seed room [of his house] an effort was made to burn the body." "The three blacks in their combined statements at the county jail . . . ," the *Star* continued, "were said to have at times even corrected each other in mentioning some detail in the murder plot and its final consummation in the murder of the planter."[16]

Circuit Judge J. I. Sturdivant convened the Kemper County grand jury in DeKalb on 4 April, and it was reported that since all "three negroes are alleged to have made full and complete confessions," it was thought that "indictments would be brought and the trio placed on trial at once." This proved to be the case, since the grand jury indicted Brown, Shields, and Ellington late in the day on 4 April, charging that the trio "on or before the 4th day of April . . . 1934 did then and there willfully, unlawfully, feloniously and of their malice aforethought, kill and murder one Raymond Stuart, a human being, contrary to the form of the statute in such cases made and provided, against the peace and dignity of the State of Mississippi."[17]

After being indicted, the three blacks were escorted from Meridian to DeKalb by officers "heavily armed with machine guns" for an arraignment. Ed Brown and Yank Ellington pleaded guilty in the arraignment before Judge Sturdivant, but Henry Shields pleaded not guilty, contending that he had not struck any of the blows that had resulted in Raymond Stuart's death. Judge Sturdivant in any case refused to accept the guilty pleas of Brown and Ellington, and instead entered pleas of not guilty for all three of the defendants and fixed the next day, 5 April, as the date for their trial. John A. Clark, Joe H. Daws, D. P. Davis and L. P. Spinks, all DeKalb attorneys, were appointed by Sturdivant as counsel for the defendants. "As soon as the blacks had been arraigned and their trials fixed, they were hurried back to Meridian" by Lauderdale County officers, the Meridian *Star* reported. "It is believed by officials . . . that if the three blacks are convicted they will be at once sentenced to be hanged at the earliest date allowed under the law. This was thought might fix the death date for Friday, May 11."[18]

Again guarded by officers armed with machine guns, Ed Brown, Henry Shields, and Yank Ellington were placed on trial as scheduled on 5 April in the Circuit Court of the Sixteenth Judicial District with Judge Sturdivant presiding. The defendants were represented by four court-appointed De-

Kalb attorneys, while the prosecution rested in the hands of District Attorney John C. Stennis. Stennis was a native of Kemper County, having been born there in August 1901. He had been educated at the Kemper County Agricultural High School at Scooba; Mississippi State College, where he received his bachelor's degree in 1923; and the University of Virginia Law School, where he received his law degree in 1928. After earning his law degree, Stennis almost immediately entered politics, representing Kemper County in the Mississippi house of representatives from 1928 to 1932. He had been elected district attorney for the Sixteenth Judicial District in 1931, and was thus in his third year as district attorney at the time of the trial.[19]

On the evening of Friday, 6 April, an all-white jury returned verdicts of guilty of murder in the first degree against the defendants, after having deliberated approximately thirty minutes. Upon the receipt of the jury's verdicts, Judge Sturdivant immediately sentenced the defendants to be hanged on 11 May 1934.[20]

"Placed on the stand to testify in their own behalf," the Meridian *Star* reported regarding the trial, "the three negroes admitted the confessions they had made to Meridian and Kemper county officers in the Lauderdale county jail but stated they were not telling them the truth, and that a promise by the officers that they would be protected prompted them to make the confessions." The performance of the court-appointed counsel for the defendants, the *Star* continued, "was such as to receive the commendation of court and spectators alike, while the prosecution conducted by District Attorney John Stennis was of a character that added to the brilliant distinction that he had already won during his administration of the office."[21]

After having been sentenced to be hanged, Brown, Shields, and Ellington were rushed back to the Meridian jail and placed in a condemned cell "to await the day of execution which will take place at DeKalb." "Quick action by Judge Sturdivant in recalling the grand jury and the trial without delay," the Meridian *Star* reported, "was said to have met the approval of Kemper citizens and any apprehension that may have been felt regarding attempted mob violence had been relieved."[22]

Only one week after the discovery of a dying Raymond Stuart, therefore, Ed Brown, Henry Shields, and Yank Ellington had been arrested, indicted, tried for murder, and sentenced to be hanged. And there appeared to be general satisfaction in Kemper County and Meridian that no lynching had occurred and that justice had been speedily administered. In an editorial, titled "Kemper Proves Itself," published after the trial, the Meridian *Star* praised the manner in which Raymond Stuart's murder had been solved and punishment meted out to those guilty of the crime. "Three negroes are sentenced to die in Kemper county in the early part of May," the *Star* said. "The three blacks are self-confessed murderers of Raymond Stuart, a prominent Kemper county cotton planter. The jury in DeKalb, after some thirty minutes of deliberation, returns a guilty verdict. Whereupon Judge J. I. Sturdivant imposes the death penalty." The case, the *Star* continued, had been "handled expeditiously—With due justice to the accused and with due consideration for the social order." Although talk of "mob violence has proven rampant," the *Star* noted, "due to the cooperation of Sheriffs Jim Adcock of Kemper, and Brice M. Stephens of Meridian, mobocracy has been eliminated and the law has taken its judicial course. Apparently, the negroes have enjoyed a fair, impartial trial. Four leading Kemper lawyers were appointed in defense," but the jury, "after hearing the confessions and all the other evidence, finds the negroes guilty. The court imposes the ultimate in penalties."[23]

"All of which appears to indicate not only the efficiency of courts, but the needlessness of 'mob' vindictiveness," the *Star* pointed out. "Centuries ago, the Mosaic law declared: 'An eye for an eye; a tooth for a tooth; a life for a life.' This Kemper county verdict serves to prove that group action is unneeded, when courts are 'on the job'—That justice is at least more certain through due 'process of law' than through the uncertainties of mass impetuosity." " 'Bloody Kemper' has redeemed itself—Proof anew that the 'bloody' appellation has never been deserved," the *Star* concluded. "Kemper proves its fundamental fairness, not through mobocracy, but through established agencies of justice. A few more like examples of swift and certain retribution—and 'rabble' illegality will disappear through the south."[24]

The Meridian *Star*'s approval of the handling of the proceedings in the aftermath of Raymond Stuart's murder reflected the feeling that the community was fortunate that mob violence had been avoided and that a trial had occurred at all. This feeling undoubtedly reflected the fact that Mississippi led the nation in the lynching of blacks in 1934, there being six reported lynchings in the state that year.[25]

A gallows was constructed at the Kemper County jail in preparation for the hanging of Ed Brown, Henry Shields, and Yank Ellington, while the three condemned men spent their days in the Meridian jail praying and singing gospel songs. The gallows at DeKalb became something of a tourist attraction and was visited by Mississippians from miles around.[26]

But whatever such visitors may have anticipated, the gallows at the DeKalb jail was never used to execute Brown, Shields, and Ellington. Despite the satisfaction expressed by the press and local officials regarding the prosecution and conviction of these three blacks, and the characterization of the proceedings against them as "fair" and in conformity with due process of law, the facts relative to what had actually transpired in the proceedings against the three blacks convicted of Raymond Stuart's murder had not been reported in the local press. What had actually occurred was one of the gravest violations of elementary standards of due process and justice that may be found in the history of American jurisprudence—violations that subsequently led a judge of the Mississippi Supreme Court to state that the transcript of the trial of Brown, Shields, and Ellington read "more like pages torn from some medieval account, than a record made within the confines of a modern civilization which aspires to an enlightened constitutional government."[27] And the proceedings against the three blacks were subsequently denounced also by the United States Supreme Court in a landmark decision regarding the rights of criminal defendants.[28]

Why the murder trial of three obscure Mississippi blacks produced such results is made obvious, not by the contemporary press accounts, but by an examination of the evidence produced at their trial.

1. Arthur M. Schlesinger, Jr., *The Coming of the New Deal* (Boston: Houghton Mifflin, 1959), pp. 375–76.

2. Arthur F. Raper and Wallis Chivers, *The Mob Still Rides: A Review of the Lynching Record, 1931–35* (Atlanta: Commission on Interracial Cooperation, 1936).

3. Dan T. Carter, *Scottsboro: A Tragedy of the American South,* rev. ed. (Baton Rouge: Louisiana State University Press, 1979), pp. 11–50. See also Jessie Daniel Ames, *The Changing Character of Lynching* (Atlanta: Commission on Interracial Cooperation, 1942).

4. Arthur F. Raper, *The Tragedy of Lynching* (New York: Negro University Press, 1969), p. 92; the population statistics on Kemper County are drawn from U.S. Department of Commerce, Bureau of the Census, Fifteenth Census of the United States, *Population Bulletin, Mississippi* (1930), pp. 5, 15.

5. Raper, *Tragedy of Lynching,* pp. 85–87.

6. Ibid., p. 88.

7. Meridian *Star,* 31 March 1934, p. 1. The Record in *Brown* v. *Mississippi* as well as many contemporary newspapers, refers to Raymond Stuart as "Stewart." The Meridian *Star,* which presumably was familiar with the name, spelled the name "Stuart," and I have followed the *Star's* version herein. Compare the Record, pp. 1–5, and the Meridian *Star,* 31 March 1934, p. 1.

8. Meridian *Star,* 31 March 1934, p. 1.

9. Ibid.

10. Ibid., 1 April 1934, p. 1, 5.

11. Ibid., 2 April 1934, pp. 1, 9.

12. Ibid.

13. Ibid., 3 April 1934, pp. 1, 9.

14. Ibid.

15. Ibid.

16. Ibid.

17. Ibid., 4 April 1934, p. 1; Record, *Brown* v. *Mississippi,* p. 1.

18. Meridian *Star,* 5 April 1934, p. 1.

19. Jackson *Daily Clarion-Ledger,* 2 Nov. 1951, p. 8.

20. Meridian *Star,* 7 April 1934, pp. 1, 7.

21. Ibid.

22. Ibid.

23. Ibid., 8 April 1934, p. 4.

24. Ibid.

25. *Literary Digest*, 119 (12 Jan. 1935): 18, reporting figures compiled by the Tuskegee Institute's Department of Records and Research.

26. Meridian *Star*, 6 May 1934, pp. 1, 2; Mrs. John A. Clark to Arthur Garfield Hays, 13 Dec. 1935, ACLU Archives, vol. 941.

27. Brown v. State, 173 Miss. 563, 574 (1935).

28. Brown v. Mississippi, 297 U.S. 278 (1936).

"Not Too Much For a Negro"

The Trial of the Kemper County Trio

The trial of Ed Brown, Henry Shields, and Yank Ellington began at 9:00 a.m. on Thursday, 5 April 1934.[1] Representing the state, District Attorney John Stennis called Burt Stuart, the brother of the slain Raymond Stuart, who presented to the jury a drawing of the layout of his brother's house. Testifying next was William Adams, one of those who discovered Raymond Stuart's body on 30 March. Stuart, Adams said, was still alive when he found him but was "breathing hard and seemed to be unconscious." Near the body was a tool chest, Adams said, "and it was open and a pair of trays were laying on top of the chest. All along the wall next to the door there was blood and blood was sprinkled in the tool chest. By this door going out to the back door there was bits of glass like a lamp chimney." Although he had summoned a doctor, Adams testified that Raymond Stuart died before the doctor arrived thirty minutes later. "From what I saw of . . . [Stuart] by the light of the lantern," said Adams, "blood almost completely covered his face, with cotton seed stuck on his face. His face looked like it was swollen. That was about all I noticed except there was blood on the seed and where he was laying."[2]

Dave Owen, the next prosecution witness, testified that he had also arrived at Stuart's home while he was still alive, but he "was breathing hard then, [and] he died after I got there. I was looking at him and he died right then. I reckon he was dying when I got in." Stuart, Owen said, had been clothed in his shirt and underwear; his shirt was scorched a little, and a broken lamp lay near the body. Keys dangled from the lock in the tool chest near the body.[3]

Two physicians had also ultimately arrived at Raymond Stuart's house, and both examined the body of the dead man. One of the doctors, a Dr. Wall of Scooba, testified that when he arrived at the murder scene the "tool chest was open, and the trays were in it, and this chisel was laid across on the top of the trays. The chisel was bloody from one end to the other. There was blood all over the tool box," and in one corner of the room there was a "big puddle of blood." "The bowl of a lamp was about a foot and a half away, and it was covered with blood," Dr. Wall continued. "The whole wick, the upper part and the lower part showed that it had been on fire," and Stuart's shirt was burned and scorched.[4]

Dr. Wall testified that Stuart had been dead for from fifteen to thirty minutes when Wall arrived, and that Stuart's body had an "intused bruise or wound on the right shoulder," the collar bone was broken, and "the shoulder joint was bursted all to pieces." "That was due," he said, "to a direct blow; it may have been aimed at his head, but that is where it hit, right on the shoulder. On account of his not dying and the circulation keeping up for some hours after he was struck there was some contusion and blueness extending from that joint up the side of his neck. I noted also that the skin was off his right cheek. I attributed that possibly to a burn and blister and in struggling on the cotton seed the skin over the blister might have been rubbed off."[5]

Stuart, Wall said, had also sustained four or five fractures of the skull, including a deep wound behind his right ear, and "there were two cut wounds behind the left ear and fractures also. There was also a deep cut around in front of the left ear that you could run your finger in plumb down to the bone." "In the top of his head," the doctor continued, "the bones were beat to jelly and there were cut wounds there you could run your finger in. When we first observed Mr. Stuart laying there, there was blood caked all over his face; you wouldn't know who he was. There was no way to identify him then."[6]

Asked by District Attorney Stennis which wounds had caused Stuart's death, the doctor testified that any of the wounds "except the wound on his shoulder could have caused his death." This was confirmed by Dr. I. W. Cooper of Meridian, who, as the next witness, testified that he too had examined Stuart's body. "I think," Cooper said, "any one of five wounds on him would have caused his death."[7]

After the testimony of the medical doctors, District Attorney Stennis called to the stand Henry Lavender, who lived near Raymond Stuart's farm and who had participated in the investigation of the murder. Lavender testified that in the course of the investigation, he and some other men had gone to the house of Henry Shields and had broken in through a window. "We went and turned up the bed and looked under the bed and couldn't find nothing," Lavender said. "We got in the kitchen, and there was a pen built in the corner of the house about three feet high," he continued. "We seen a pile of clothes in there and looked in them and down about that deep in the clothes we found a jumper. We pulled it out and seen gray hairs on it. I said: 'Don't you reckon this is hog hair?' We taken it to the light, and they said: 'No, this is human.' We spread it out and looked and found blood on the jumper in the front on both arms and also all over the back, and there was some slobber on the back and gray hairs." "That was where they had hit him on the head, I suppose," Lavender said, "and knocked the hair out."[8]

District Attorney Stennis asked Lavender whether or not in his opinion the gray hair on the jumper found at Henry Shields's house was human hair, and Lavender replied in the affirmative. Lavender also testified, in response to questioning by Stennis, that he had been personally acquainted with Raymond Stuart, and that his hair had been gray. The jumper was then admitted as evidence to be considered by the jury.[9]

In response to further questions from Stennis, Lavender testified that he had subsequently returned to Henry Shields's house, because he had heard that Shields possessed an ax. "I went and looked in the house, and it was not there," Lavender said. "Then I went out to the wood pile and got to looking and found the axe in the wood pile with two sticks of wood over it . . . and the handle was sticking out." "I picked the axe up . . . and laid it on a stick of wood and looked on it and found blood. The axe looked like it had been freshly washed; you can see on the top there the rust where it was freshly washed." "Wait a minute," Stennis interrupted. "At the time you found it, state whether or not the blood on it appeared to be fresh blood." "Yes, sir. . . ," Lavender responded.[10]

Crucial to the prosecution's case against Brown, Shields, and Ellington were of course the confessions they had made to various officers while incarcerated in the Meridian jail, and District Attorney Stennis next called as a witness Kemper County sheriff J. D. Adcock, who had been among those who had heard the confessions. "Mr. Adcock, down in the Meridian jail last Monday afternoon or night, did you have a conversation with either one of these defendants concerning the death of Mr. Raymond Stuart?" Stennis asked. At this point, however, L. P. Spinks, one of the defense attorneys, objected and moved that the question of the admissibility of Sheriff Adcock's testimony be determined in the absence of the jury. The court sustained the objection, and the jury retired while the judge considered the question.[11]

The question explored in the absence of the jury was whether the confessions that Brown, Shields, and Ellington had allegedly made had been completely free and voluntary as required by Mississippi law, a question Sheriff Adcock answered in the affirmative under questioning by both District Attorney Stennis and defense counsel. Sheriff Adcock testified in response to questions by Stennis that at first he had talked to each of the defendants separately and that he had assured them that he and the other officers at the jail were determined to protect them from any mob violence. He had not promised the defendants any immunity from prosecution, Adcock said, and indeed had warned them that they would have to pay the price for their acts under the law. No threats or intimidation of any kind had been used during his interrogation of Brown, Shields, and Ellington, the sheriff assured the court, and at the end of the interrogation, after each had confessed to the murder of

Raymond Stuart, "one or possibly more said that we dealt very kindly with them. They said to me that I didn't even look like I was mad." And in fact, Adcock added, both Ellington and Brown had stated to him at the outset of the trial that their confessions had been the truth.[12]

Adcock was then cross-examined by John A. Clark. He again denied that he had threatened force against any of the defendants, and stated that although he had not warned them that what they said might be used against them, he had warned them that they might hang for the murder of Stuart. Each of the defendants had nonetheless freely and voluntarily confessed to the murder, Adcock testified, and although he had heard that they had also previously confessed, he did not know of the circumstances under which the previous confessions had been obtained. Asked by Clark whether any of the defendants had complained about their treatment prior to his interrogation, Adcock admitted that Henry Shields "came in limping, and he kind of got on the box easy and looked like he was excited. I said: 'Henry, sit on that box,' and he said: 'I can't; they strapped me pretty hard.' I said: 'Make yourself comfortable; nobody is going to hurt you at all. All of us are here for your protection.'" "Did you understand that the confession that he had already made was brought about by putting him on a box and using a strap on him?" Clark asked. "I didn't understand anything about how it might have happened, but he stated that he couldn't sit down," Adcock responded. Despite Shields's statement, the sheriff had not inquired further into the matter.[13]

At the conclusion of the cross-examination, Judge J. I. Sturdivant ruled, over John Clark's objection, that the confessions of Brown, Shields, and Ellington were admissible as evidence before the jury, and the jury was thereupon summoned back to the courtroom to hear Adcock's testimony. Under questioning by District Attorney Stennis, the sheriff explained that at first he questioned the defendants individually and then brought them together to make their statements. On the afternoon of the day of the murder, Adcock said the trio had informed him, they had met and discussed the fact that Ellington and Brown had not received checks for their cotton, which Raymond Stuart owed them. Henry Shields had agreed to join Brown and Ellington that evening, Adcock said, for the purpose of killing Stuart and taking the money they believed he kept in his house. They had broken into Stuart's house, the sheriff continued, and attacked Stuart as he slept, hitting him first with a stick and an ax, but Stuart fled into the hallway adjoining his bedroom, where the attack continued. Ed Brown had broken into a tool chest in the house, and used a "foot-ax" obtained from the chest to bludgeon Stuart until he fell against the tool chest.[14]

After Stuart had been beaten unconscious, Adcock testified, Ed Brown used the keys to Stuart's safe and opened it, as well as a closet, in search of money. However, he found nothing. Ellington and Shields then carried Stuart's body to a room used to store cotton seed, while Brown poured the oil from a lamp on and around the body and on the cotton seed and threw the lighted wick from the lamp into the cotton-seed storeroom in an attempt to burn the body and the house.[15]

After they had confessed to the murder of Stuart, Adcock testified, Brown, Shields, and Ellington indicated that they were relieved to have confessed the truth. "I asked them if they had told the truth and all the truth, and they said that they had," the sheriff told the court. "This little boy on the end, Ellington, I believe he was smiling. He said: 'Yes, sir. I feel a whole lot better.' He asked one of the gentlemen there for a cigarette. I said: 'Any man who tells the truth feels better.' I said: 'What about you, Ed?' and he said, 'Yes, sir, I feel a heap better.' I said: 'What about you, Henry?' and he wouldn't answer. The others said they had told us what licks they hit," Adcock said, but Shields denied hitting Stuart at all.[16]

Sheriff Adcock also identified a set of keys introduced into evidence by District Attorney Stennis as being the keys that were dangling from the lock of the tool chest at Raymond Stuart's house. In their confessions, Adcock testified, Ellington and Shields had said that Ed Brown customarily carried the keys in connection with his duties on the Stuart farm, and that he had used them to unlock a safe and a closet in the Stuart house in his search for money. Although Adcock was cross-examined by L. P. Spinks and Joe H. Daws on behalf of the defense, the cross-examination was perfunctory and did not discredit Adcock's testimony upon direct examination.[17]

B. M. Stephens,[18] the sheriff of Lauderdale County, was called as the next prosecution witness. Again defense counsel objected to any testimony regarding confessions by the defendants on the ground that such confessions had not been free and voluntary. Judge Sturdivant again overruled this objection, and Sheriff Stephens was allowed to testify. Like Sheriff Adcock, Stephens denied that the confessions of Brown, Shields, and Ellington resulted from threats or violence. "I told them they were in my care and keeping and I was going to protect them even at the cost of my own life," he said. "I told them that I wanted any statement that they made to be free and voluntary on their part." Stephens then related the confessions that he had heard from the defendants, and his testimony was virtually identical to that of Sheriff Adcock. Like Adcock, Stephens was subjected to only cursory cross-examination by defense counsel.[19]

Finally, Rev. Eugene Stephens, the brother of Sheriff Stephens, was called as a prosecution witness and testified that he had been present at the Meridian jail when the defendants had confessed. Rev. Stephens confirmed the versions of the confessions as testified to by Adcock and Stephens, and he also denied that any force or threats had been used to obtain the confessions. The defendants had been "told that [the officers] were there to protect them," he said, "and were going to see that they had a fair trial and for them to feel easy." The defense again objected to Rev. Stephens's testimony, but again Judge Sturdivant overruled the objection, and with that, the prosecution rested its case.[20]

With the resting of the case for the prosecution, a dramatic change occurred at the trial, and the benign picture of kindly law enforcement officers interested only in voluntary and truthful confessions and the protection of those in their custody was starkly contradicted by the testimony of Ed Brown, Henry Shields, and Yank Ellington as witnesses in their own behalf. Testifying first on behalf of the defense, Ed Brown stated that he had been born in Sumter County, Alabama, was thirty years old, and had a wife and three children, aged five, ten, and thirteen. He had worked as a tenant on Raymond Stuart's farm for three years, he said, and had never had any difficulties with Stuart. Stuart had "treated me nice," he said, "and I done the same thing."[21]

In response to questions by defense counsel John Clark, Brown denied that he had been telling the truth in the statements he had made to Sheriffs Adcock and Stephens while in custody at the Meridian jail. He had confessed, Brown said, only after he had been subjected to brutal whipping at the hands of Kemper County deputy sheriff Cliff Dial, and he had repeated the confession to Adcock and Stephens the following day only because he had been threatened with further torture if he did not do so.[22]

On the Sunday evening after the murder of Raymond Stuart, Brown testified, he was in custody in the Meridian jail when Deputy Sheriff Dial had come to his cell and had told him that he had heard that Brown had said that he had killed Stuart. Brown denied to Dial that he had participated in the murder, but Dial had said, "Come on in here and pull your clothes off; I am going to get you." Three men had whipped him with a strap with buckles on the end, Brown continued, with Dial doing most of the whipping. "They stripped me naked and bent me over a chair, and I just had to say it; I couldn't help it," Brown told the court. "Did you bleed any?" John Clark asked. "Did I bleed? I sure did," Brown replied. "How did you tell about the light and the lamp and such things as that?" Clark asked. "They whipped me so hard, and I said I didn't know anything about them, and they put me down the third trip and said, 'Ain't that so?' He said: 'What about the lamp?' and I said: 'I reckon Henry Shields done that.' They said: 'You know more than that.' They put me down again, and they whipped me so hard I couldn't sleep that night."[23]

He had repeated the confession thus beaten from him on the following day to Adcock and Stephens, Brown testified, only because he was afraid of further beatings. Adcock and Stephens had not threatened him, he admitted, but Deputy Sheriff Dial had warned him that he had better repeat the confession he had given as a result of the beatings. "That is the reason you told Mr. Adcock what you did?" John Clark asked.

"Yes, sir, that is the reason," Brown responded. "If you could see the places [on his body as a result of the beating], you would say a train didn't move any lighter."[24]

Under further questioning by John Clark, Ed Brown testified that contrary to his confession, he and his wife had visited a neighbor the night of the murder of Raymond Stuart, and had returned home and gone to bed around 10:00 p.m. The first two times he had been whipped, he said, he had steadfastly refused to admit any participation in Stuart's murder, saying, "I ain't never harmed Mr. Stuart in my life." When the whipping was repeated for the third time, Brown said, "it looked like he was going to kill me, and I said: 'Yes, sir.' He said: 'What about the lamp?' I said: 'I don't know.' He said: 'Put him down again,' and I said, 'Yes, sir.' He was whipping me so hard I had to say 'yes, sir.' "[25]

Under cross-examination by District Attorney Stennis, Brown admitted that he had later repeated the confession thus extracted from him to Kemper County sheriff Adcock, and that on that occasion he had not been subjected to any threats or violence. And he also admitted having told Adcock as the trial began that his confession had been truthful. But Brown maintained that his confession to Adcock and his subsequent statement that the confession had been truthful were the result of his fear that he would be subjected to further beatings unless he adhered to the confession beaten from him. "The man whipped me so I had to say it," Brown said. But the truth was that "I ain't never harmed Mr. Raymond. There ain't no need of saying I done it when I didn't." "If I die right now," he continued, "I am going to say it: I ain't never harmed Mr. Raymond in my life. If they want to they can kill me because I said that, but I ain't ever harmed Mr. Raymond in my life."[26]

Fear of further beatings, Brown maintained on Stennis's cross-examination, had been the reason he had confessed to the murder and had even pleaded guilty when he had been arraigned before Judge Sturdivant. "Didn't you know it would hang you when you told that you killed . . . [Stuart]?" Stennis asked, and Brown acknowledged that he understood the consequences of his confession. "But you went on and told that [to Sheriffs Adcock and Stephens] on Monday night?" Stennis persisted. "Yes, sir," Brown replied. "I was scared because . . . [Deputy Sheriff Dial] beat me so." "And you told it again today?" Stennis continued. "I was still scared," Brown insisted. "Are you scared now?" Stennis asked. "Yes, sir," Brown responded, concluding his testimony.[27]

Henry Shields was called as the next defense witness. He testified that he was twenty-seven years old and married. The night of the murder, he claimed, he had had a fight with his wife and had left home and gone to Meridian, where he was arrested by Kemper County deputy sheriff Cliff Dial and other officers on Saturday afternoon, March 31. He had been lodged in the Meridian jail, Shields said. In response to questions by defense counsel Joe H. Daws, as to whether he had had any trouble at the jail, Shields answered in the affirmative. He had encountered a "whipping spell," he said. "Mr. Cliff tore me up."[28]

On Sunday evening, Shields continued, Cliff Dial came to the jail and whipped him until he confessed to the murder of Raymond Stuart. "First I tried to tell the truth," he testified, "but he wouldn't let me. He said: 'No, you ain't told the truth,' and I tried to stick to it. He whipped so hard I had to tell him something. He said: 'Ed Brown done told that you helped kill Mr. Raymond.' I said: 'No, if there is a God in Heaven, I ain't had nothing against Mr. Raymond. He could be home walking around as far as I know.'"[29]

Two other men were present when he was whipped by Dial, Shields testified, and the whipping was so severe that "blood ran through my pants, and I had them washed and then commenced bleeding again." He had confessed to the murder in the presence of Sheriffs Adcock and Stephens, Shields said, only because Dial had warned him that if he changed his story he would be beaten again. "'Henry, if you don't tell them folks the same thing you told us, I will get meat again,'" Dial had warned. "I had rather you all would kill me," Shields told the court, "than let Mr. Cliff get me again."[30]

Finally, Arthur Ellington testified in his own behalf that he was twenty years old, was married, and had two children, ages two and six months. He had been born and reared in Noxubee County, Alabama, and had worked for Raymond

Stuart for two years. On the night of the murder, Ellington said, he had been home in bed with his wife. On the evening of the day Stuart's body had been discovered, he continued, white men came to his house and took him to the Stuart place where he was tied to a tree and flogged by the mob that had gathered after news of the murder spread. The mob had also tied a rope around his neck, Ellington testified, and twice hanged him from a tree limb in an attempt to force him to confess to Stuart's murder. When he refused to confess, however, he was released and told "to go home, and I just could get home."[31]

The following day, Ellington said, he was taken into custody by Deputy Sheriff Cliff Dial, accompanied by Russell Dudley, and taken to the jail at Meridian. On the trip to Meridian, he said, Dial and Dudley drove into Alabama, stopped the car, and beat him until he confessed to participating in the murder of Raymond Stuart. "Did they whip you pretty bad?" John Clark asked Ellington. "Yes, sir," Ellington replied, "this side is swollen as tight as I don't know what." "Did they get any blood?" Clark inquired. "Yes, sir," Ellington said, "I have got a bandage on it now."[32]

On cross-examination, District Attorney Stennis pointed out to Ellington that he had pleaded guilty at the arraignment, but Ellington maintained that he had done so, just as he had confessed originally, because he was afraid of further beatings. Had he also been afraid of Sheriff Adcock, to whom Ellington had also confessed, Stennis asked. "Yes, sir," Ellington replied. "I am scared of all white people."[33]

The defense also produced further witnesses in an attempt to prove the innocence of Brown, Shields, and Ellington. Ellis Lee Giles testified that he had been at Henry Shields's house the night of the murder playing cards, and Mary Shields testified that she and Henry had had a fight the night of the murder and he had left home. They had scuffled over an ax, she said, and her leg had been cut during the scuffle. As for the bloody jumper found in their house, Mary Shields said that her mother had given her some fresh meat wrapped in the jumper, which had been discarded by her father.[34]

Kate Ellington, the wife of Yank Ellington, also confirmed his testimony that he had been at home in bed the night of the murder. Testifying regarding the beating and hanging of her husband at the Stuart place, Kate Ellington stated that when he returned home he "was beat pretty bad." Under cross-examination, she conceded that after the crowd at the Stuart place had beaten and hanged Yank, Deputy Sheriff Cliff Dial had finally intervened and persuaded the crowd to allow Yank to go home.[35] And Irena Brown, the wife of Ed Brown, confirmed her husband's testimony that they had visited a neighbor on the night of the murder of Raymond Stuart. They had visited Fannie Little's house, she testified, and returned home, eaten roasted sweet potatoes, and gone to bed.[36]

The fact that Brown, Shields, and Ellington had repudiated their confessions in their testimony at the trial and had alleged that their confessions had been obtained through physical brutality apparently came as a surprise to District Attorney Stennis, since he made the somewhat unusual move of reopening the case for the prosecution by calling rebuttal witnesses to the stand. By calling the rebuttal witnesses, Stennis sought to refute the testimony of the Kemper County trio that the content of their confessions had been dictated to them during the course of the beatings by which the confessions had been obtained. Stennis was therefore seeking to demonstrate to the court and jury that however the original confessions might have been obtained, the content of the confessions was truthful, and the confessions to Sheriffs Adcock and Stephens, which the defendants had admitted were uncoerced, were therefore believable.

Scooba marshal T. H. Nicholson and E. L. Gilbert both testified as rebuttal prosecution witnesses. Each denied that any suggestions had been made to Ed Brown or Henry Shields regarding what their murder confessions should contain. But during the course of their cross-examination by defense counsel, both Nicholson and Gilbert freely admitted that Brown and Shields had been beaten until they confessed. "The defendants Ed Brown and Henry Shields had been whipped before the statements were obtained?" defense counsel Joe H. Daws asked Nicholson. "They had been whipped some, yes, sir," Nicholson replied. "They were whipped two or three times before any confessions were made at all?" Daws persisted.

"No, they were only whipped once," Nicholson said. "That was in the jail in the city of Meridian, and you were present at the time? Who else was present there?" Daws continued. "Cliff Dial and Guy Jack, Warren Campbell and myself when Henry was whipped; we four went in there, and Buddy Gilbert was there when Ed was whipped," Nicholson responded.[37]

E. L. Gilbert similarly admitted that he had been present at the jail when Brown and Shields had been whipped, but denied that he had been physically present in the room when Shields was being whipped, although, he admitted, it "sounded like whipping." "When you asked Ed after he was whipped and during the time he was being whipped, you asked him about whether or not he used the ax?" Joe Daws inquired. "I asked him what he used," Gilbert said. The whipping of Brown had lasted about an hour and a half, Gilbert continued, and Brown "was whipped one time, but I don't know how many intervals there were. We told him any time he wanted to talk, we would let him up, and he got up." "There were two or three intermissions or skips between the whippings?" Daws inquired. Gilbert replied in the affirmative and said that at the conclusion of the whipping, Brown "told the same thing Henry told."[38]

In their testimony regarding the beatings to which they had been subjected, Brown, Shields, and Ellington had all identified Kemper County deputy sheriff Cliff Dial as the person primarily responsible for the beatings. Dial appears to have been a personal friend of Raymond Stuart, since he served as an honorary pall bearer at Stuart's funeral.[39] Called as a rebuttal prosecution witness, he too freely admitted that the beatings had occurred, while denying that the three blacks had been instructed as to what story to tell.

On direct examination by District Attorney Stennis, Dial stated that he had intervened after Yank Ellington had been hanged from a tree and flogged by the crowd that had gathered at Raymond Stuart's house after the murder had been discovered. "I told them that Mr. [Burt] Stuart had asked me to take charge of the place," he said, "and I didn't want any of the negroes beat up and that I didn't believe this negro was guilty and I would rather they wouldn't beat him up." When he

subsequently arrested Yank Ellington, however, Dial admitted
that he himself had whipped him during the trip to the Meridian jail. "On the way down there," Stennis asked, "did you
strap him some?" "Yes, sir," Dial replied. "He denied . . .
[committing the murder]. He said that Ed and them were in it
but that he stood around and held the light, and then he finally
told what I thought was the truth about the thing."[40]

On cross-examination by defense counsel John A. Clark,
Dial related that about twenty men had seized Yank Ellington
and whipped him at the Stuart place after the murder was
discovered. "Did they hang him there?" Clark asked. "Well,
you know they didn't hang him," Dial replied. "They pulled
him up but they didn't hang him." "Of course, they didn't kill
him?" Clark continued. "No, sir," Dial said. Dial also again
pointed out that he had tried to dissuade the mob from flog-
ging Ellington and other blacks at the Stuart place, but that he
had been unsuccessful. Had Ellington and other blacks been
whipped a "right smart" by the mob, Clark inquired. *"Not too
much for a negro,"* Dial responded; *"not as much as I would
have done if it was left to me* [emphasis added] ."[41]

After Yank Ellington had been whipped and hanged, Dial
testified, Yank had said that he had seen Ed Brown kill Raymond Stuart. John Clark then inquired whether, given the
treatment Ellington had received, he would not have been
willing to admit killing Stuart himself. "I don't think so," Dial
replied. "I think he would have had better sense than that."
Under continued questioning by John Clark, Dial again admitted that he had beaten a confession from Ellington during
the trip from Kemper County to Meridian after Ellington had
been taken into custody. "What did you say you did to him on
the way to Meridian?" Clark asked. "We stopped on the way
and got water and stopped over there and talked to him about
the thing," Dial said, "and then we strapped Yank a little bit."
"He admitted it himself after he had been strapped?" Clark
continued. "Yes, sir . . .," Dial responded. As in the case of
Yank Ellington, Dial admitted that Ed Brown and Henry
Shields had denied participating in Stuart's murder, but had
changed their stories after being beaten. "We kind of warmed
them a little—not too much," Dial testified. "But they didn't

say it until after you warmed them up?" Clark asked. "No, sir . . .," Dial admitted.[42]

John Clark later admitted that the Kemper County trio's attorneys offered only an anemic defense on their behalf and had been largely going through the motions of defending their clients. At no stage of the trial was this more evident than at the conclusion of Cliff Dial's testimony, since at that point it had become obvious from the testimony of the prosecution's own witnesses that the confessions of Brown, Shields, and Ellington had not been free and voluntary but rather were the products of physical coercion. The proper course for defense counsel would have been to move that Judge Sturdivant exclude the illegally procured confessions as evidence in the case, but no such motion was made by counsel for the defense.

The only objection offered by defense counsel was to the testimony of the rebuttal witnesses, repeating what Brown, Shields, and Ellington had said in their confessions, and this objection was sustained by Judge Sturdivant. "The only purpose of this testimony [of the rebuttal witnesses] and the only part I admit," Judge Sturdivant ruled, "is that these parties, witnesses and others, didn't suggest to these defendants at that time what they should say with regard to how it happened, nor whom they should implicate and further that they were not told to stick to this tale." And he instructed the jury that it should "disregard any part of this testimony . . . except that they didn't suggest to them what weapons were used and who was implicated and didn't tell them to stick to this tale. The other is excluded."[43]

The effect of this ruling, however, was not only to exclude the testimony of the prosecution's rebuttal witnesses regarding the content of the Kemper trio's confessions but also to exclude the testimony confirming that the trio had been beaten into confessing. Defense counsel's actions therefore resulted in the exclusion of testimony that the Kemper trio's confessions had indeed been the product of coercion, while their failure to move the exclusion of the confessions on that ground was a plain dereliction of their duty to their clients—a dereliction that almost cost Brown, Shields, and Ellington their lives.

Further damaging the case for the defense was the testimony of T. D. Harbour as a rebuttal prosecution witness. Harbour testified that he had been performing fingerprint work for the Meridian police department for eleven years and that he had found fingerprints on the smashed lamp that had been discovered next to Raymond Stuart's body. "There are two prints here that go with Ed Brown's card," Harbour said, "one is his right fore-finger and the other is his left fore-finger." "You are certain that the print that you got off the lamp is the same as the prints that you took from Ed Brown?" District Attorney Stennis asked. "Yes, sir," Harbour replied.[44]

Defense Attorney John A. Clark objected to the admission of Harbour's testimony, arguing that the prosecution had previously rested its case and that it was unusual procedure to allow the prosecution to reopen its case after having rested. Clark also pointed out that the defense had not had time to secure fingerprint experts who might be able to rebut Harbour's testimony. John Stennis, on the other hand, argued that he had been informed that the defendants had confessed and had assumed that the fingerprint evidence would therefore not be needed as part of the prosecution's case. The "State was therefore taken by surprise with the defense presented by the defendants," consisting of the repudiation of their confessions, Stennis said. Judge Sturdivant overruled the objection of the defense and allowed Harbour's testimony to be admitted, but he assured defense counsel that he would give them time to obtain their own fingerprint experts. No such attempt, however, was apparently ever undertaken by defense counsel.[45]

The final witnesses for the prosecution in rebuttal included L. G. Temple, who testified that he had visited Raymond Stuart's house on one occasion when Stuart had to send for Ed Brown to obtain from him the house keys, including the key to his safe.[46] And Dr. Wall testified that the blood on the jumper obtained from Henry Shields's house had been fresh when he had first seen it. There was no testimony, however, that the blood was of Raymond Stuart's blood type.[47]

After the prosecution rested its case in rebuttal, Judge Sturdivant instructed the jury, and at the request of defense counsel included in his instructions the admonition that "a confession solicited by threats or coercion or force or intimidation is not legal evidence and if you have any reasonable doubt the so-called confessions of the defendants resulted from threats, coercion, force or intimidation and are not true then you are not to consider same as evidence against the defendants."[48] The jury nonetheless returned verdicts of guilty of murder in the first degree, and Judge Sturdivant thereupon ruled that Ed Brown, Henry Shields, and Yank Ellington "shall be confined, or in the enclosed yard of such Prison or in such Building or enclosed yard that the Board of Supervisors of [Kemper] County may designate and there be hanged by the neck until [each] is Dead, Dead, Dead. Which execution shall be on Friday the 11th day of May A.D. 1934."[49]

After Judge Sturdivant imposed the death sentence, Brown, Shields, and Ellington were hurriedly escorted by heavily armed officers to the jail in Meridian. They were given no time to consult with their attorneys regarding any appeal, and since all three were indigent, an appeal appeared to be highly unlikely. "Confined in condemned cells at the county jail since their conviction and death sentence," the Meridian *Star* reported less than a week before the execution date, "the three blacks have spent almost all their daylight hours in praying and singing religious songs. By nightfall, becoming exhausted, they have slept apparently well, according to Jailer A. E. McGee, who has them in charge. . . . They are said by Jailer McGee to have eaten their meals regularly and heartily." And, the *Star* noted, the trio continued to maintain their innocence.[50]

1. The transcript of the proceedings, as printed in the Record, *Brown v. Mississippi,* pp. 5, 78, indicates that the trial was held on 25 and 26 March 1934. This is clearly erroneous, since Raymond Stuart was not murdered until March 30.

2. Record, *Brown v. Mississippi,* pp. 5–9.

3. Ibid., pp. 10–11.

4. Ibid., pp. 13–14.

5. Ibid., p. 14.

6. Ibid., p. 15.

7. Ibid., pp. 16–17.
8. Ibid., pp. 18–19.
9. Ibid., p. 19.
10. Ibid., pp. 19–20.
11. Ibid., pp. 20–21.
12. Ibid., pp. 21–22.
13. Ibid., pp. 23-24.
14. Ibid., pp. 25–27.
15. Ibid., pp. 27-28.
16. Ibid., p. 32.
17. Ibid., pp. 32–34.
18. Sheriff Stephens's name is spelled "Stevens" in the Record, but contemporary newspaper accounts report his name as "Stephens," and I have used the latter spelling herein.
19. Record, *Brown v. Mississippi*, pp. 34–38.
20. Ibid., pp. 38–41.
21. Ibid., pp. 41–43.
22. Ibid., pp. 43-44.
23. Ibid., p. 43.
24. Ibid., p. 44.
25. Ibid., p. 45.
26. Ibid., pp. 45–51.
27. Ibid., pp. 51–55.
28. Ibid., pp. 58–59.
29. Ibid., p. 59.
30. Ibid., pp. 59–61.
31. Ibid., pp. 68–70.
32. Ibid., pp. 70-72.
33. Ibid., p. 76.
34. Ibid., pp. 80, 87–90.
35. Ibid., pp. 82–83.
36. Ibid., pp. 84–85.
37. Ibid., pp. 99–102.
38. Ibid., pp. 103–6.
39. Meridian *Star*, 31 March 1934, p. 3.
40. Record, *Brown v. Mississippi*, pp. 107–8, 111.
41. Ibid., pp. 111–12.
42. Ibid., pp. 112–14.
43. Ibid., p. 103.
44. Ibid., pp. 91–93.
45. Ibid., pp. 78–80.
46. Ibid., p. 98.
47. Ibid., p. 115.
48. Ibid., p. 124.
49. Ibid., p. 4.
50. Meridian *Star*, 6 May 1934, pp. 1, 2.

3

John Clark's Appeal

The proceedings against Ed Brown, Henry Shields, and Yank Ellington in Mississippi in 1934 were remarkably similar to the proceedings that had occurred in the Scottsboro, Alabama case in 1931. In both, black defendants were charged with especially heinous crimes in the eyes of the white South—rape of white women in the Alabama case and murder of a white man in the Mississippi case. Mob violence had also appeared to be imminent in both cases, and the black defendants were subjected to hasty indictments and trials amid assurances by the press to the public that if mob violence were eschewed, justice would be done. And the proceedings in Scottsboro, Alabama, and Kemper County, Mississippi, produced the same melancholy results—death sentences for the defendants—while both communities congratulated themselves because mob violence had been avoided and the forms of the law had been observed.[1]

However, the proceedings against the Kemper County trio received no early publicity outside of Mississippi, whereas the Alabama Scottsboro litigation had soon generated national and even international attention. The publicity regarding the Scottsboro litigation was at least initially attributable to the fact that two national organizations—the National Association for the Advancement of Colored People (NAACP) and the International Labor Defense (ILD)—attempted to intervene on behalf of the Scottsboro defendants and engaged in an increasingly vitriolic exchange of charges and countercharges, as each organization battled for control of the litigation.[2]

The NAACP was founded in 1909 by a small group of blacks and whites to combat what they regarded as the "new slavery" being imposed upon American blacks, who were being denied the right to vote and were being subjected to mob violence, lynchings, and increasingly rigid policies of racial segregation. Litigation on behalf of the rights of blacks soon became a principal activity of the NAACP, and by the 1930s the association had won important victories in the U.S. Supreme Court regarding residential segregation[3] and the denial of the right to vote to blacks through "grandfather" clauses and the white primary.[4]

The NAACP's litigation activities had also produced notable results with regard to the rights of criminal defendants under the Due Process Clause of the Fourteenth Amendment, as a consequence of the U.S. Supreme Court's 1923 decision in *Moore* v. *Dempsey*. In the *Moore* case, the association came to the defense of a group of black sharecroppers and tenant farmers who had been convicted of murder and sentenced to death in Philips County, Arkansas, in 1919. The NAACP was able to demonstrate that white planters had attacked blacks in Phillips County who were attempting to organize a tenant farmers union, and that when some whites were killed in the ensuing melee, twelve blacks were prosecuted and convicted of murder and sentenced to death, while sixty-seven others were sent to prison.

The record in the *Moore* case revealed, however, that the black witnesses who testified against the twelve condemned men had been severely beaten to force them to testify, and that the courthouse at which the trials were held had been dominated by a mob. In the *Moore* case, the NAACP sued in federal court to attack the validity of the conviction of some of the condemned Phillips County blacks, arguing that the trials in the Arkansas courts had violated the Due Process Clause of the Fourteenth Amendment and that the federal court should order the release of the condemned men through its power to issue writs of habeas corpus to vindicate federally protected rights.

Although the federal trial court ruled against the NAACP, the U.S. Supreme Court reversed the trial court, ordering it to hold a habeas corpus hearing, and, if there had indeed been mob domination of the trials of the condemned blacks, to order their release. Speaking for a majority of the Supreme Court, Justice Oliver Wendell Holmes said that "if the case is that the whole proceeding is a mask—that counsel, jury, and judge were swept to the fatal end by an irresistible wave of public passion, and that the state courts failed to correct the wrong,—neither perfection in the machinery for correction nor the possibility that the trial court and counsel saw no other way of avoiding an immediate outbreak of the mob can prevent this court from securing to the petitioners their constitutional rights."[5]

As a result of the litigation in the *Moore* case, the NAACP was able to win the release of not only all twelve of the Arkansas blacks who had been condemned to death but also all of the men imprisoned in the wake of the trouble in Phillips County.[6] From the standpoint of constitutional development, however, the more important consequence of the NAACP's victory in *Moore* v. *Dempsey* was that the U.S. Supreme Court for the first time had restricted, via the Due Process Clause of the Fourteenth Amendment, the freedom of the states to conduct criminal trials as they saw fit. Despite the fact that the forms of a trial were observed by the states, the Court appeared to be saying in the *Moore* case, if in fact defendants were being denied the essence of a fair trial, as was the case if the trial were mob dominated, then, under the Due Process Clause, the Court would reverse the convictions thus obtained. The increased willingness of the Supreme Court to look behind the mere forms of the proceedings in state criminal trials and to inquire as to whether in fact a fair trial had been afforded criminal defendants, which was first evident in the *Moore* decision, subsequently proved to be extremely important to the defendants in the Scottsboro litigation as well as to the Kemper County trio in Mississippi.[7]

In contrast to its rather spectacular victory in the *Moore* case, the NAACP was less successful in its attempts to defend the nine black youths convicted of rape and sentenced to death in the Scottsboro case. The association was slow to react to the Scottsboro case and failed to win the support of the parents of the defendants. As a result, control of the Scottsboro litigation was wrested from the NAACP by the ILD. And in the organizational battle over control of the Scottsboro litigation, which lasted throughout much of the 1930s, the NAACP's reputation as the leading defender of the rights of blacks was damaged; furthermore, the association's ineptness at the outset of the litigation subjected it to criticism in non-Communist, liberal circles.[8]

Organized in 1925 by the Communist Party as a front group, the International Labor Defense perceived the Alabama litigation to involve not only the fate of the black youths who had been convicted at Scottsboro but also the oppression of the working class by the capitalist class through the capitalist-controlled courts. While challenging the death sentences of the Scottsboro defendants in the courts, the ILD therefore additionally used the litigation as a propaganda weapon both in the United States and abroad as part of the Communist Party's attack upon capitalism. Litigation to free the Scottsboro defendants was necessary, the ILD conceded, but the ILD and the Communists also contended that the courts were "instruments of national and class oppression," and that litigation must be subordinated to the "development of revolutionary mass action outside of courts and bourgeois legislative bodies." Only mass action by the black and white working class, the ILD and the Communists maintained, would ultimately free the Scottsboro defendants.[9]

The ILD therefore arranged tours for the mothers of the Scottsboro defendants. It organized rallies and meetings that produced a torrent of publicity about the case as well as thousands of letters, telegrams, and petitions addressed to Alabama officialdom denouncing the Scottsboro proceedings. The Scottsboro defendants had been railroaded to the electric chair by the "brutal slave drivers of Alabama acting through a Ku Klux Klan judge," a typical letter received by Alabama officials said, and the death sentences for the defendants were an attempt by the "white ruling classes" to attack "the Negro masses and the working class as a whole."[10]

The tactics of the ILD and the Communists in the conduct of the Scottsboro litigation, and their violent denunciation of any individual or organization that would not accept their tactics and their control of the litigation, had the effect of alienating individuals and groups who were sympathetic to the Scottsboro youths and who otherwise would have contributed to their defense. This was especially true of the NAACP, which, having lost the battle with the ILD for control of the litigation, formally withdrew from the case in 1931 amid charges by the ILD that the association had "helped the southern lynchers in the murder of nine Negro boys."[11]

The methods pursued by the Communists and the ILD in the conduct of the Scottsboro litigation also alienated moderate and progressive forces in the South which might otherwise have acted on behalf of the defendants. One such force was the Commission on Interracial Cooperation (CIC), which had been founded in 1919 by prominent Southern whites and blacks in response to the rise in racial tensions after World War I, tensions that led to the "red summer" of race rioting during 1919. Headquartered in Atlanta and composed of rather conservative members of the black and white Southern elite, the CIC did not attempt to challenge the system of racial segregation but rather addressed itself to defusing explosive racial tensions on an ad hoc basis, while also attacking the grossest manifestations of racism in the South. The CIC thus concerned itself with such issues as the more accurate portrayal of blacks in the press and the improvement of such services as sewers, street paving, and lighting and of social and welfare services for the black community. The commission also engaged in a vigorous program in opposition to lynching and peonage, and it furnished legal aid in selected cases involving particularly egregious examples of discrimination against or intimidation of members of the Southern black community.

The key figure in the Commission on Interracial Cooperation was Dr. William W. Alexander, who became the director of the commission at its founding and remained in that capacity for twenty-five years. Born in 1884 in Missouri and educated at Scarritt-Morrisville College and Vanderbilt University, where he received a divinity degree in 1912, Alexander left the Methodist ministry during World War I to work with the YMCA. At the age of thirty-five, he became the CIC's director and driving force. "Dr. Will," as he was affectionately called, was extremely effective in attracting funding for the CIC, and grants from the YMCA, the Phelps-Stokes Fund, the Rockefeller Laura Spellman Fund, the Carnegie Corporation, and the Julius Rosenwald Fund enabled the commission to spend more than two and a half million dollars during its existence between 1919 and 1944.[12]

Describing the work of the CIC, Will Alexander pointed out that the commission "never had any creed." "We didn't have any doctrine of any kind," he continued. "We assumed that there was a job to be done in a great many communities that could not be done except if it were done under the leadership of the whites and the colored working together. We didn't tell them what to do. We told them to find their own problems and work together at them. If there was anything radical about it, it was that for the first time whites and Negroes sat down together as citizens."[13]

Critics of the CIC, on the other hand, noted that the commission never attacked the system of racial segregation that lay at the heart of the system of injustice to blacks in the South. Indeed, as one critic has said, in "attempting to soften and humanize segregation as it was practiced in the South during the 1920s and 1930s, the commission in effect sanctioned the idea of the Southern Negro as a second-class citizen."[14] However justified such criticism may have been, the CIC was virtually the only organization of Southerners that was dedicated to the improvement of racial relations in the region during the 1920s and '30s.

The CIC had an active branch in Alabama when the Scottsboro case arose, but the members of the Alabama Interracial Commission joined in the general self-congratulation common in Alabama and the South generally for the fact that the Scottsboro defendants had not been lynched. The middle- and upper-middle-class whites who composed the Alabama Interracial Commission were alarmed by the intervention of the ILD and the Communists in the Scottsboro litigation, and they were convinced that these "outside," Northern radical groups were falsely portraying the Scottsboro trials as unfair for propaganda purposes.

The Alabama Interracial Commission therefore adopted a hands-off attitude toward the Scottsboro litigation and charged that there was "brilliant leadership, sleepless energy and apparently unlimited money behind the malevolent [Communist] activity. . . . Race hatred, race discord, murder, rape [and] lynchings" were the Communists' "immediate object." The ILD was using the case as "an opportunity to make propaganda," Will Alexander agreed, and had begun "world-wide agitation under the assumption that it was part of the class struggle," when in fact it was not, "and the interference of the Communists . . . injects into the case elements which make it very difficult to get adequate defense for the boys."[15]

As John B. Kirby has noted, Will Alexander, and probably the CIC movement in the South as a whole, perceived racial harmony in the South to be threatened by white segregationist extremists on the one hand and black militancy on the other,[16] and the tactics pursued by the ILD and the Communists in the Scottsboro case appeared to Alexander and the interracial movement to play into the hands of both extremes. And when a black tenant farmers' union was organized apparently under Communist auspices in Tallapoosa County, Alabama, and armed clashes between whites and black union members occurred near Camp Hill in the summer of 1931, the apprehension of Alexander and other members of the interracial movement seemed to be confirmed. "If we can escape violence on a large scale," Alexander said, "or a break between white and colored people in the next two or three years, we shall be very fortunate."[17]

Further alienating the liberal and moderate southerners in regard to the Scottsboro case was the fact that the ILD and the Communist Party openly advocated racial equality and attacked the system of racial segregation that had become a way of life in the South since Reconstruction. As George B. Tindall pointed out, the "key to acceptance" in the South of even the modest efforts at interracial cooperation promoted by Will Alexander and the CIC "was avoidance of the segregation issue." The advocacy of "social equality" by the ILD and the Communists thus further assured a lack of support for the Scottsboro cause by Southern moderates and liberals, since supporters of the Scottsboro case risked being labeled not only as pro-Red but as allies of radical "outsiders" attacking the Southern way of life.[18]

Despite the fact that their tactics tended to alienate support from liberal and moderate non-Communist individuals and groups, the ILD and the Communists managed to raise over eleven thousand dollars to defend the Scottsboro defendants by the end of 1932, making it possible to appeal the first Scottsboro case, *Powell* v. *Alabama*, to the U.S. Supreme Court.[19] And the Supreme Court's decision in the *Powell* case on 7 November 1932 reversed the convictions of the Scottsboro youths on the ground that they had been denied a fair trial in violation of the Due Process Clause of the Fourteenth Amendment.

On the day the Scottsboro defendants were tried, the trial judge had appointed all members of the bar present in the courtroom as counsel for the defendants, but this, the Supreme Court held in the *Powell* case, was insufficient to afford them the effective assistance of counsel. The Due Process Clause, the Court held, required the states to afford criminal defendants a fair trial, and the trial and conviction of ignorant black youths for the capital offense of rape without effective representation by counsel on their behalf denied the right to a fair trial or hearing mandated by the Due Process Clause.

The Court had held in *Moore* v. *Dempsey* in 1923 that the Due Process Clause required the states to afford criminal defendants fair trials in fact as well as form. And in *Powell* v. *Alabama*, the Court expanded the *Moore* fair-trial rule to include the right to effective assistance of counsel, since the right to a fair trial or hearing, the Court said, "would be, in many cases, of little avail if it did not comprehend the right to be heard by counsel." Due process therefore required, the Court held, that the states must appoint counsel for indigent defendants in capital cases, and even in noncapital cases if the lack of counsel would result in an unfair trial for a defendant.[20]

Although the ILD achieved an important victory with the Court's path-breaking decision in *Powell* v. *Alabama,* the vehemence of the attacks upon Alabama and its officialdom instigated by the Communists during the Scottsboro litigation led to a climate of almost hysterical fear of radical influences in the state as well as a hardened resolve to defend the initial results in the Scottsboro case.[21] Despite evidence that the white women the defendants were alleged to have raped were prostitutes and that they had not in fact been raped, Alabama authorities continued to prosecute the defendants. New convictions secured in the Alabama courts were again reversed in 1935 by the U.S. Supreme Court on the ground that Alabama's jury selection system involved systematic discrimination against blacks,[22] but Alabama authorities persisted in retrying the defendants. By 1937, however, many Alabamians, including much of the state's press, were conceding that the Scottsboro litigation had long since become a monumental embarrassment to the state, and four of the defendants were finally released by the state. The remaining five defendants escaped the death penalty, but still served long prison sentences.[23]

The tragic history of the Scottsboro litigation held several lessons for any one who sought to defend black criminal defendants accused of crimes against whites in the South during the 1930s, and it therefore had special salience to any possible further defense proceedings regarding Ed Brown, Henry Shields, and Yank Ellington, who awaited execution in Mississippi. First, it was clear from the Scottsboro case that any defense of Southern black defendants by an organization perceived in the South as radical—especially if the organization was an "outside," Northern group advocating "social equality" for blacks—would be met with virtually monolithic opposition, even by Southerners otherwise liberal to moderate in their racial attitudes. The organization of publicity campaigns in which a state and its officialdom were held up to criticism and vilification in the Northern press was also contraindicated by the history of the Scottsboro case. The fate of the defendants would ultimately be held in the hands of state courts and state officials, and the effect of negative campaigns appeared to only harden the resolve of state authorities to defend their own honor as well as that of their state from outside attack.

If Southern moderate to liberal individuals and groups, as well as the press and officialdom, were not to be alienated, therefore, the Scottsboro experience indicated that the best strategy for the defense of black defendants was to focus narrowly upon the alleged injustice that had occurred in the specific case at hand. Such a strategy necessarily entailed the elimination of any perception that the defense efforts were part of a broad-gauged attack upon "the Southern way of life," the system of racial segregation, the South as a region, or the specific state involved. Little if any publicity should be deliberately generated by the defense, this strategy indicated, and ideally the defense efforts should be led by Southern lawyers, since the employment of Northern lawyers by the ILD in the Scottsboro litigation had also been a source of deep resentment in Alabama.[24]

Although the tactics of the ILD and the Communists in the Scottsboro case thus suggested an alternative strategy for the defense of black defendants in the South, the tactics pursued in the Alabama case had nevertheless created an advantage for defense efforts in such cases in the future. For largely as a result of the activities of the ILD and the Communists, Alabama and its officialdom had been held up to criticism, vilification, and eventually ridicule for a period of years because of the Scottsboro case, and many Alabamians had suffered profound embarrassment. Urging the governor to pardon the Scottsboro defendants in 1938, Grover Cleveland Hall, editor of the Montgomery *Advertiser*, declared, "I do not know whether they are guilty or innocent of the rape of two cut-rate prostitutes. I do not care. . . . The fact is that the character of Alabama and its people is at stake before the world."[25] With Alabama's experience in the Scottsboro case in mind, it therefore was not unreasonable to predict that the leadership in most Southern states would seek to avoid being subjected to the same kind of embarrassing ordeal. And this factor was to the advantage of future defense efforts on behalf of Southern black defendants, since obdurate opposition to such defense efforts seemed less likely after the Scottsboro experience as the leadership of other Southern states sought to escape the fate of Alabama.

With regard to the case of Ed Brown, Henry Shields, and Yank Ellington, however, considerations regarding the most effective defense strategy appeared to be largely irrelevant as the three men awaited the date of their execution in the Meridian jail in May 1934. For unlike the Scottsboro case, no organizations immediately intervened to organize a defense of the Kemper County trio, and no parades, rallies, or publicity barrages were organized around their case. The fate of Brown, Shields, and Ellington in 1934 rested not in the hands of the NAACP, the ILD, the CIC, or any other organization, but in the hands of one man—John A. Clark, of DeKalb.

Serving as a court-appointed attorney on behalf of the Kemper trio, John Clark had only reluctantly defended them at the trial and had been initially convinced of their guilt. The revelations at the trial of the torture to which the Kemper trio had been subjected, however, effected a change in Clark's attitude toward the three blacks. Indeed, the experience of the trial appears to have seared John Clark's conscience, and he subsequently played a crucial role in saving Brown, Shields, and Ellington from the gallows.

Clark, along with L. P. Spinks, was appointed by Judge J. I. Sturdivant as defense counsel at the arraignment of the Kemper County trio on 4 April, but Clark was ill and asked to be excused from acting as defense counsel. Judge Sturdivant refused his request, and this was a major turning point in the case, since if Clark had been excused as defense counsel, Brown, Shields, and Ellington would almost certainly have been hanged.[26] At the arraignment, however, one of the defendants stated to Judge Sturdivant that they "just as well plead guilty," and Clark learned from the officers present that the trio had confessed. In addition to being ill, therefore, Clark concluded that he was being saddled with the defense of clients who were plainly guilty of a heinous crime and who should be convicted by the jury. As Clark said later, he and Spinks, as well as Joe H. Daws and D. P. Davis, who were also appointed defense counsel on the day of the trial, were not "at all in sympathy with the defendants," but were in fact prejudiced against them "and thought they should be convicted." Having heard from the officers that the defendants "had voluntarily confessed to the murder," Clark said, he had "at that time no doubt of their guilt and was simply going through the form of a trial."[27]

Clark's mind was changed on this score, however, by the manner in which the trial was conducted and the revelation of the torture to which the defendants had been subjected. Judge Sturdivant had been in such a hurry to complete the trial of the Kemper County trio, Clark later said, that he did not allow defense counsel adequate time to confer with their clients. On the day of the arraignment, when he and L. P. Spinks were appointed as defense counsel, Clark said, the two attorneys were allowed to confer with their clients for only thirty or forty minutes before the latter were whisked back to Meridian. The trial itself began the following morning, at which time Joe H. Daws and D. P. Davis were appointed as additional defense counsel, but again the defense attorneys and Brown, Shields, and Ellington were allowed to confer only for an hour or two before the trial began.

As defense counsel and the defendants entered a room in the courthouse for this brief conference, Clark said, Kemper County deputy sheriff Cliff Dial attempted to enter the room too, and when this was objected to, Dial stood outside the door and listened at the keyhole. Within a short time, Clark continued, "not exceeding thirty or forty minutes, a messenger was sent into the room by the court with the statement made to us that the court . . . [did] not want to unduly hurry you gentlemen in your conference with the defendants, but to get through as quickly as you can, as the court desires to proceed with the trial, and in the course of an hour or two spent in the conference, the court sent two or three times with this message to the defendants' counsel to hurry them up with the conference." After Judge Sturdivant had pressed them to hurry, Clark continued, the defense attorneys decided to proceed with the trial, but because of the circumstances under which counsel had conferred with the defendants, there had been no opportunity to obtain witnesses favorable to the defense or even to learn much about the case against the defendants.[28]

The fact that Brown, Shields, and Ellington had been tortured, Clark also noted, was evident from the wounds on their bodies that anyone who encountered them could see. Yank Ellington, Clark said, had "his neck all scarred up with a ring around it that could be observed clear across the court room." After the defendants had testified how they had been beaten by those eliciting their confessions, Clark continued, defense counsel could "see why the ignorant negroes were in such desperate fear of Mr. Dial, and that they had upon their bodies tremendous sores and stripes placed there by the whippings and this was brought to the attention of the court and the district attorney and the jury in open court." Nevertheless, after defense counsel had made a "feeble argument" to the jury on behalf of the defendants, the jury shortly returned a verdict of guilty against the Kemper trio.[29]

Immediately after Judge Sturdivant had pronounced sentence upon Brown, Shields, and Ellington, they were hurriedly escorted back to Meridian. The result was, Clark pointed out, that there was "no opportunity to make a motion for a new trial, it being dark on the night of [April] 6th, no money [was] in the hands of anybody to pay for going down there [to Meridian] to visit them or have any talk with them, and without their having been brought back or given any opportunity to make a motion for a new trial or confer with counsel about making one." Indeed, on the morning of 7 April, Clark said, Judge Sturdivant signed the minutes of the trial and adjourned the court for the term, thus effectively preventing any motion for a new trial from being made.[30]

Although Clark was conscience-stricken after the trial of the Kemper County trio, many factors militated against his taking any further action in the case. As he had pointed out, any further legal action on behalf of the defendants would have to go uncompensated, since the trio were indigent. And, although Mississippi law required that appointed counsel for indigent individuals be compensated at the rate of twenty-five dollars per client, Judge Sturdivant refused to authorize such payments to Clark and the other defense attorneys, apparently fearing public reaction in Kemper County to any such action on his part.[31] Clark also consulted with L. P. Spinks, Joe H. Daws, and D. P. Davis, who had served with him as defense counsel, regarding the possibility of an appeal in the case. Spinks and Daws refused to "have anything to do with any effort at appeal" in the case, Clark said, while Davis was willing to allow the use of his name in an appeal, but refused to actively participate in any further proceedings.[32]

Given the emotions aroused by the murder of Raymond Stuart in Kemper County, Clark undoubtedly considered also the consequences to his own career of any further actions on his part on behalf of Brown, Shields, and Ellington. Clark was fifty years old at the time of the trial, and he had what was apparently a promising future in Mississippi politics before him. He had served as the Democratic committeeman from the Fifth District for sixteen years before being elected to the state senate, representing Kemper and Winston counties, in 1927. Winning reelection to the senate in 1931, Clark was serving as the senate floor leader under the administration of Governor Sennett Conner at the time of the trial of the Kemper County trio. Clark's wife, Matilda Floyd Tann Clark, was also active politically and was well connected in Mississippi politics. At the time of the trial, she was serving as the Democratic national committeewoman from Mississippi, and her brother was the superintendent of the Mississippi state penitentiary, while her brother-in-law was Judge George H. Ethridge of the Mississippi Supreme Court.[33]

Any further action by John Clark on behalf of Brown, Shields, and Ellington would undoubtedly prove to be exceedingly unpopular in Kemper County and would probably jeopardize both Clark's and his wife's political futures. Indeed, one of the Clarks' closest personal and political friends, Judge Marion W. Reily of Meridian, advised them that John Clark would be "wasting his time on a losing cause" by proceeding further in the case of the Kemper County trio. Reily was considered one of the state's leading criminal lawyers, and he informed Mrs. Clark that her husband "was too valuable and greatly needed in Mississippi public affairs to be permitted to sacrifice his life for three negroes."[34]

Reily's advice may be understood only by taking into

account the dominance of the politics of racial prejudice in Mississippi during the 1930s. Mississippi had led the way among the Southern states in disfranchising blacks with its adoption in 1890 of a literacy test and poll tax as voting requirements. "All understood and desired," one delegate to the 1890 constitutional convention said, "that some scheme would be evolved which would effectively remove from the sphere of politics in the State the ignorant and unpatriotic negro."[35] The literacy test and poll tax eliminated Mississippi blacks as voting participants in the politics of the state, but the mere existence of the large black population in the state resulted in a politics in which racial prejudice played a substantial role.[36]

Mississippi politics was thus dominated in the first half of the twentieth century by such figures as James K. Vardaman, popularly called the "Great White Chief," and Theodore G. Bilbo. Serving as governor and U.S. Senator from Mississippi, Vardaman, and later Bilbo, refined the demagogic exploitation of racial prejudice to a fine art. Vardaman campaigned on a platform calling for the repeal of the Fifteenth Amendment (which, theoretically at least, guaranteed blacks the right to vote) and the modification of the Fourteenth Amendment. He also opposed any public expenditures for the education of blacks, saying, "Why squander money on his education when the only effect is to spoil a good field hand and make an insolent cook." The black person, Vardaman assured white Mississippians, was a "veneered savage."[37]

The Vardaman tradition of racial demagoguery was continued by Theodore Bilbo, who was elected governor of Mississippi in 1915 and again in 1927 and who was elected to the U.S. Senate in 1934, the year the Kemper County trio were tried. Bilbo, one of his enemies declared, "was a pert little monster, glib and shameless, with that sort of cunning common to criminals which passes for intelligence." "The people loved him," the description continued. "They loved him not because they were deceived in him but because they understood him thoroughly; they said of him proudly, 'He's a slick little bastard.' He was one of them and he had risen from obscurity to the fame of glittering infamy—it was as if they themselves had crashed the headlines."[38]

During Bilbo's first term as governor, Eugene Green, a

black man, was lynched at Belzoni, Mississippi, in 1919. The National Association for the Advancement of Colored People inquired of Bilbo as to the circumstances surrounding the lynching, and in response, playing upon the association's name, Bilbo said, "[Eugene Green] . . . was 'advanced' all right from the end of a rope, and in order to save burial expenses his body was thrown into the Yazoo river." An adamant opponent of federal antilynching legislation, Bilbo denounced a proposed antilynching bill on the floor of the U.S. Senate in the late 1930s, inquiring "what Senator . . . will not understand that the underlying motive of the Ethiopian who has inspired this proposed legislation, the antilynching bill, and desires its enactment into law with a zeal and a frenzy equal if not paramount to the lust and lasciviousness of the rape fiend in his diabolical effort to despoil the womanhood of the Caucasian race, is to realize the consummation of his dream and ever-abiding hope and most fervent prayer to become socially and politically equal to the white man."39

But Bilbo's prejudices and intolerance were not visited upon blacks alone; they were directed at other religious and ethnic groups as well. Answering accusations that he was guilty of racial and religious intolerance, he once declared that he was for "every damn Jew from Jesus Christ on down." Responding to a critical letter sent to him as U.S. Senator by an Italian-American woman, he addressed his reply to "My dear Dago." Bilbo, U.S. Senator Robert A. Taft declared, was "a disgrace to the Senate."40

Since he lived in a state that conferred many of its highest political rewards upon racist demagogues such as Bilbo and Vardaman, John Clark could not have been blamed for hesitating before taking up the cause of three blacks who were convicted murderers of a white man. Despite the possible consequences, and the fact that he continued to be physically ailing, Clark decided to perfect an appeal to the Mississippi Supreme Court on behalf of Ed Brown, Henry Shields, and Yank Ellington. On 5 May, less than a week before the trio were scheduled to be hanged, Clark traveled from DeKalb to Meridian and interviewed the three blacks in the Meridian jail. Because of the "manner and haste in which the trial was conducted," Clark said, he "went at his own expense down to Meridian, and had a conference with each of the defendants and was so impressed . . . with their innocence" that he decided to file an appeal in their case.[41]

Although he had made the decision to appeal the case of the Kemper County trio to the Mississippi Supreme Court, John Clark still faced the problem that there was no money to finance the appeal. Consequently, Clark took another step that, had it been publicly known in Mississippi, would have been exceedingly unpopular—he informed the National Association for the Advancement of Colored People of the situation and appealed to the association for financial aid.[42]

Since the NAACP had met defeat at the hands of the International Labor Defense regarding control of the Scottsboro litigation, the association might reasonably have been expected to be sensitive to cases raising issues similar to those in the Scottsboro case and to have quickly thrown its resources into the Kemper County case. This, however, the association did not do, apparently because, unlike the Scottsboro case, the trial of the Kemper trio had not received national publicity and thus the NAACP had not been informed of the case through the media. Also, the association typically relied heavily upon local contacts and local branches for information, but there was no active local NAACP branch anywhere in Mississippi, and no individual blacks in Mississippi had taken it upon themselves to inform the NAACP of the plight of Ed Brown, Henry Shields, and Yank Ellington. When John Clark appealed to the NAACP for financial aid in appealing the case of the Kemper County trio to the Mississippi Supreme Court, the association sent him a small check in July 1934, but took no further action regarding the case pending the outcome of the appeal.[43]

John Clark was therefore largely on his own, financially and otherwise, in conducting the appeal to the Mississippi Supreme Court. And in structuring his arguments for the reversal of the convictions of Brown, Shields, and Ellington, Clark made an error that came perilously close to costing his clients their lives. That error consisted of his failure to challenge the convictions of the Kemper County trio under the federal Constitution in his appeal to the Mississippi Supreme

Court. Clark instead based the appeal entirely upon questions arising under Mississippi law, with the result that, if the Mississippi Supreme Court affirmed the convictions, there would be no basis upon which to appeal to the United States Supreme Court.[44]

Under Mississippi law, a successful attack upon the convictions of the Kemper County trio would have to overcome some serious problems. The principal argument made by John Clark on appeal was of course that the confessions admitted as evidence against Brown, Shields, and Ellington had been the products of coercion, and that the convictions of the defendants should thus be reversed since they were based on incompetent, inadmissible evidence. And a 1887 decision of the Mississippi Supreme Court appeared to strongly support Clark's argument on this point.

In *Ellis* v. *State,* the state supreme court had ruled that when the admission of a defendant's confession was objected to at trial on the ground that it had not been free and voluntary, the trial judge should excuse the jury and hold a hearing on the admissibility of the confession. If at this hearing outside the presence of the jury, the trial judge concluded that the confession was free and voluntary, then the jury should be permitted to hear it, the supreme court held. This, of course, was the procedure followed in the trial of the Kemper County trio, and Judge Sturdivant had ruled the confessions of Brown, Shields, and Ellington to be admissible after a hearing with the jury excused.[45]

However, the Mississippi Supreme Court had further held in the *Ellis* case that even if the trial judge ruled a challenged confession to be admissible as competent evidence, "either party has a right to produce before the jury the same evidence which was submitted to the court when it was called upon to decide the question of competency, and all other facts and circumstances relevant to the confession, or affecting its weight or credit as evidence; and if it should be made to appear at this point, or any other, during the progress of the trial, that the confession was made under such circumstances as to render it incompetent as evidence, it should be excluded by the court."[46]

If the *Ellis* decision had stood alone, the prospects for a reversal in the case of the Kemper County trio on appeal would have appeared to be favorable, since the Mississippi Supreme Court seemed to have held in the *Ellis* case that an initial determination by a trial judge that a confession was admissible was not conclusive. Rather, the court seemed to be saying, evidence and testimony during the course of a trial could lead to a reversal of the earlier decision to admit a confession, since the subsequent evidence and testimony could lead to a conclusion that the confession had not in fact been free and voluntary. And if this occurred, it was the duty of the trial court to exclude the confession, despite an earlier favorable ruling on its admissibility.

Despite Judge Sturdivant's initial ruling in the trial of Brown, Shields, and Ellington that their confessions were admissible, the subsequent testimony in the trial had indicated that the confessions had been in fact the products of coercion. The *Ellis* case thus appeared to indicate that Judge Sturdivant should have excluded the confessions from consideration by the jury once the evidence of coercion had developed during the course of the trial, and his failure to do so was reversible error under Mississippi law.

Unfortunately for John Clark and the Kemper County trio, however, the *Ellis* decision had been significantly modified in *Loftin* v. *State*, decided by the Mississippi Supreme Court in 1928.[47] Hines Loftin, a black youth, was implicated in the murder of his stepfather, and was interrogated by a group of whites numbering from twenty-five to seventy-five persons, some of them armed, for several hours before being taken into custody by the county sheriff. At Loftin's trial for murder, several of the whites who had interrogated him testified, at a hearing conducted by the trial judge in the absence of the jury, that Loftin's confession during the interrogation had been free and voluntary. On the basis of such testimony, the trial judge ruled that Loftin's confession had not been coerced and admitted it as evidence for consideration by the jury. Testifying in his own defense subsequently, however, Hines Loftin stated that his confession had been induced by those interrogating him through fear and promises of leniency.

Under the Mississippi Supreme Court's decision in the *Ellis* case, defense counsel could have moved the exclusion of Loftin's confession at this point at his trial, since his testimony regarding the circumstances under which it had been elicited indicated that it had not been free and voluntary, contrary to the trial judge's initial conclusion with respect to its admissibility. Loftin's counsel nevertheless failed to request that the trial judge exclude his confession, and in affirming Loftin's conviction for murder, the Mississippi Supreme Court subsequently held that counsel for the defense were required to object to or move to exclude allegedly inadmissible confessions during the trial, since otherwise the supreme court would find no reversible error had occurred by reason of the admission of such confessions and their consideration by trial juries.

The Mississippi Supreme Court pointed out in the *Loftin* case that "no request was made of the [trial] court to exclude the confessions after the introduction of testimony which it is now claimed tended to show that the confessions were inadmissible." "In the introduction of his proof, on the merits," the court continued, "the appellant offered testimony which it is now claimed tended to show that the confessions were made under the influence of hope or fear, but after the introduction of this testimony no motion was made to exclude the confessions. If, as contended, this testimony tended to show that the confessions were inadmissible. . . , the court committed no error in not excluding them, in the absence of a request to do so."[49]

The reasoning of the majority of the court was rejected by Judge William Dozier Anderson, who forcefully dissented from the ruling in the *Loftin* case. Born in Pontotoc County in 1862, Anderson had received his education at Central University in Richmond, Kentucky, and the University of Mississippi Law School. After his admission to the bar in 1883, he served as Lee County attorney for several years and subsequently as city attorney, alderman, and, for ten years, mayor of Tupelo. Anderson was elected to the state supreme court in 1921, and was in his sixty-sixth year when the *Loftin* case was decided.[49]

Hines Loftin, Judge Anderson pointed out in his dissent, had been interrogated at night "with his hands tied behind him, in the presence of from 25 to 75 white people who had gathered around him, some with guns. Imagine a negro making a voluntary confession of the crime of murder under such circumstances and surroundings, especially in view of the well-known nature and characteristics of the negro, and his relations with the white race!" The "very atmosphere of the situation, it seems to me," Judge Anderson said, "showed that the confession was the result of fear—the fear of being mobbed. The crowd surrounding . . . [Loftin] in the nighttime, with guns in the hands of some of its members, must have looked to him like a mob. Can it be said that the requirement of the law, that the evidence must show beyond a reasonable doubt that the confession was free and voluntary, was complied with? I think not."[50]

Despite Judge Anderson's dissent, however, the ruling in the *Loftin* case indicated that under Mississippi law, if testimony or evidence presented during a trial indicated that a confession had been coerced, the confession would not be excluded from consideration by a jury unless defense counsel specifically objected and moved to exclude it. And, in the trial of the Kemper County trio, defense counsel had not objected to the jury's consideration of the confessions of Brown, Shields, and Ellington after the testimony at the trial had indicated that the confessions had been coerced. In arguing for a reversal of the convictions of the Kemper trio because their confessions had been coerced, John Clark thus faced a serious problem in the *Loftin* case, a problem that ultimately proved to be insuperable.

The appeal on behalf of the Kemper County trio was argued by John Clark before the Mississippi Supreme Court on 26 November 1934, while Assistant Mississippi Attorney General William D. Conn, Jr., represented the state. Some six weeks later, on 7 January 1935, the supreme court rendered its decision affirming the convictions of Brown, Shields, and Ellington and upholding the death sentences they had received in the Kemper County court.[51]

The court noted that when the confessions of Brown, Shields, and Ellington were about to be admitted as evidence by the prosecution through the testimony of the Kemper

County sheriff, defense counsel had objected and a hearing on the admissibility of the confessions was held in the absence of the jury. During this hearing, the Kemper County sheriff testified, the supreme court pointed out, "that he assured each of the defendants that he would protect them from harm from outside sources, that no threats of violence were made against them, no force or intimidation used, and no hope or promise of reward or inducements of any kind held out to them; that they were repeatedly admonished to tell only the truth, and that the statements were freely and voluntarily made."[52]

Counsel for the defense, the court said, had cross-examined the sheriff, but had not offered any evidence to contradict his testimony that the confessions of the Kemper County trio had been free and voluntary. The cross-examination by defense counsel, the court conceded, had produced testimony by the sheriff that he had heard rumors that the Kemper trio had been previously whipped and had confessed, and that Henry Shields had limped into the room in which the confessions were heard by the sheriff and had stated that he could not sit down because he had been strapped pretty hard. The sheriff, on the other hand, had warned the three blacks that they could be hanged for the murder of Raymond Stuart, and they had acknowledged that they were aware of that fact.[53]

Upon the basis of this testimony, the supreme court continued, the trial judge had ruled the confessions to be free and voluntary and allowed testimony as to the contents of the confessions to go to the jury. After Brown, Shields, and Ellington repudiated their confessions on the witness stand and testified regarding the beatings to which they had been subjected, the court said, the prosecution had reopened its case and called rebuttal witnesses who denied the allegations of the defendants that the contents of their confessions had been dictated by those administering the beatings. But in the course of the examination of these rebuttal witnesses, the court admitted, "it was developed that before the . . . [Kemper trio] made the first statements they had been whipped." On motion of defense counsel, the court nevertheless pointed out, all of the testimony of these rebuttal witnesses was excluded by the trial court, except that which stated that the contents of the defendants' confessions had not been suggested to them. "No other request in reference to the testimony of these witnesses," the supreme court noted, "was made of the court."[54]

The principal error justifying the reversal of the convictions of Brown, Shields, and Ellington presented to it by John Clark, the court said, was that the confessions of the defendants should not have been admitted as evidence at their trial because they were the products of coercion. Judge Sturdivant had correctly permitted testimony regarding the confessions in his initial ruling on their admissibility, the court held, since there was at that point in the trial no evidence before the court indicating that the confessions were other than free and voluntary. With the testimony of the defendants repudiating their confessions and the testimony of the prosecution's rebuttal witnesses, the court conceded, "there was testimony which stongly tended to show that the confessions were made under the influence of fear induced by threats and violence, but no motion was made to exclude the confessions." After Judge Sturdivant's initial ruling admitting the confessions of the Kemper trio as evidence, the judge had never thereafter been called upon by defense counsel to exclude them, the court pointed out, "and as held in the case of Loftin vs. State . . . , wherein identically the same circumstance and situation were presented, 'the court committed no error in not excluding them, in the absence of a request so to do.' "[55]

In the *Loftin* case, the court continued, "it was expressly held that if a confession has been properly admitted in evidence after a preliminary examination as to its competency, no error is committed by a failure to exclude it, in the absence of a request so to do, although during the later progress of the trial it is made to appear that the confession was made under such circumstances as to render it incompetent as evidence." "The Loftin Case is applicable and controlling here, and in the absence of error on the part of the lower court in failing to exclude the confessions we cannot reverse upon that point," the supreme court concluded. "The judgment of the court below will therefore be affirmed, and Friday, February 8th, 1935, is set as the date for the execution of the sentence."[56]

As he had in the *Loftin* case, Judge William D. Anderson

vigorously dissented from the ruling of the Mississippi Supreme Court. The evidence produced at the trial, he argued, "showed without any substantial conflict that the . . . [Kemper trio] were driven to confess their guilt by most brutal and unmerciful whippings and beatings at the hands of persons who doubtless thought they were guilty." And if the confessions of Brown, Shields, and Ellington had been excluded, as they properly should have been, Anderson asserted, "the evidence was wholly insufficient to sustain the conviction." Contrary to the conclusion of the majority of his colleagues, Anderson contended that even Judge Sturdivant's initial ruling admitting the confessions as evidence at the trial had been erroneous, since the Kemper County sheriff had admitted during the preliminary inquiry regarding the admissibility of the confessions that Henry Shields had entered the room limping and had stated that he had been strapped so hard that he could not sit down. Even Adcock's testimony at the preliminary inquiry, Anderson therefore argued, was insufficient to demonstrate that the Kemper trio's confessions had been free and voluntary beyond a reasonable doubt and to a moral certainty.[57]

The evidence produced at the trial proved "without material conflict" that the confessions had been obtained by brutal whippings, Anderson continued, but defense counsel had not subsequently renewed their initial objections to the admission of the confessions as evidence. It appeared that the initial objections by defense counsel should have been sufficient to put the court on notice that there was a continuing defense objection to the admission of the confessions, Anderson said, but "if wrong about that, should the general rule laid down in the controlling opinion govern in this case? It is a common saying that there are exceptions to all rules. If that be true, this is one case that ought to come within the exception." "Wipe out these confessions, and the court would have been forced to direct a verdict of not guilty," Anderson declared. "The court had staring it in the face this incompetent testimony without which there could be no conviction. Must the lives of the . . . [Kemper trio] be taken by law because their counsel failed to bring to the attention of the court this incompetent evidence? Are they without remedy?"[58]

Judge Anderson further argued that, leaving aside questions arising under Mississippi law, the proceedings against the Kemper County trio should be condemned under the Due Process Clause of the Fourteenth Amendment of the U.S. Constitution on the basis of the U.S. Supreme Court's decision in *Powell* v. *Alabama.* "Viewing this trial as a whole," he said, "it appears to me that it is condemned by the principles laid down by the Supreme Court of the United States in the Scottsboro cases." The due process guarantee of a right to a fair trial in a capital case had been construed by the U.S. Supreme Court in the *Powell* case to require the effective assistance of counsel for the accused, he pointed out, and Brown, Shields, and Ellington had not been afforded this right at their trial. The Kemper trio had been subjected to a hurried trial at which their attorneys had failed to object to the admission of confessions that had been beaten from them, Anderson charged, and without "the confession the evidence was wholly insufficient to convict."[59]

"In some quarters there appears to be very little regard for that provision of the bill of rights [of the state constitution] guaranteeing persons charged with crime from being forced to give evidence against themselves (Section 26 of the Constitution)," Judge Anderson concluded his dissent. "The pincers, the rack, the hose, the third degree, or their equivalent, are still in use."[60]

While none of his colleagues on the Supreme Court of Mississippi joined him in dissent, Judge Anderson's dissenting opinion was nonetheless of considerable importance to the defense of Brown, Shields, and Ellington, since it was the first public condemnation of the treatment to which the Kemper trio had been subjected in the proceedings against them. And that condemnation had come not from "outside" individuals or organizations, but from a respected figure in the Mississippi political establishment—a judge of the state supreme court. Judge Anderson's dissent therefore conferred a measure of respectability and legitimacy upon defense efforts on behalf of the Kemper trio, and by suggesting that the trio's convictions were invalid under the U.S. Supreme Court's decision in the first Scottsboro case, *Powell* v. *Alabama,* Anderson was the first to suggest that the convictions of Brown, Shields, and

Ellington might appropriately be reversed by the U.S. Supreme Court.

Notwithstanding Anderson's eloquent dissent, John Clark had lost the appeal to the Mississippi Supreme Court, and the court shortly issued a formal order affirming the Kemper trio's convictions. And the court also directed that "Ed Brown, Henry Shields and Yank Ellington, for their crime of murder, be safely kept in the jail of Kemper County until Friday, February 8th, 1935, and on that day between the hours of 10 o'clock A.M. and 4 o'clock P.M. within the jail yard of Kemper County or at such other convenient place as the Board of Supervisors of Kemper County may designate, the said Ed Brown, Henry Shields and Yank Ellington, be by the Sheriff of Kemper County, hanged by their necks until they are dead."[61]

"Three Kemper Negroes to Die," was the headline in the Meridian *Star* reporting the decision of the state supreme court. The *Star* quoted extensively from both the majority opinion and the dissent by Judge Anderson, with the result that for the first time readers of that newspaper were informed of the allegations that the Kemper trio had been subjected to brutal whippings to force them to confess. Raymond Stuart's murder, the *Star* also noted, "was one of the most brutal in the history of Kemper county."[62]

The supreme court's affirmation of the convictions of Brown, Shields, and Ellington, and Judge Anderson's strongly worded dissent, also led to publicity regarding the case in the press at Jackson, the state capital. Both the Jackson *Daily Clarion-Ledger* and the Jackson *Daily News* quoted sizable excerpts from the majority and dissenting opinions in their reports on the decision.[63] Unlike the Meridian *Star,* the Jackson *Daily News* had reported the allegations that the Kemper trio had been whipped as a part of its coverage of their trial,[64] but the *Daily News* also noted in its report of the state supreme court's decision that Raymond Stuart's "murder was one of the most repulsive in recent state history, and feeling was high before and after the trial."[65]

The Kemper County trio thus faced execution by hanging within less than a month after the state supreme court's decision, and it appeared that all possible remedies in their case had been exhausted. John Clark had not raised any federal questions in their case by alleging that the proceedings against them had violated the federal Constitution. Therefore no appeal to the U.S. Supreme Court was possible in the posture the case was in after the state supreme court's decision, despite Judge Anderson's suggestion that the Kemper trio's convictions had violated the principles enunciated in *Powell* v. *Alabama.*

Clark nevertheless appears to have been oblivious to the problem an appeal to the U.S. Supreme Court would present, since he informed the NAACP of the Mississippi Supreme Court's decision and indicated that he hoped to appeal the case to the U.S. Supreme Court. The NAACP, however, was in a precarious financial condition because of the Depression, with the result that there was little the association could do to help either Clark or the Kemper trio. Roy Wilkins, the NAACP's assistant secretary, noted in his diary Clark's request for assistance and somewhat helplessly expressed the hope that the NAACP "can help, as it looks like a bad case, but we have so little money."[66]

Despite John Clark's initial enthusiasm for an appeal to the U.S. Supreme Court, the intense pressure to which he was subjected in Kemper County because of the case began to take its toll, and he subsequently wrote the NAACP indicating that he was increasingly convinced that his participation in the case had become personally dangerous. "I believe these men have been tortured to make them confess and that confession is the only evidence against them," Clark informed the NAACP, "but I cannot carry this case any further. It's so bad that I think it would be well if your organization would come in and help them." The leadership of the NAACP—secretary Walter White, assistant secretary Roy Wilkins, and board of directors' chairman Louis Wright—discussed the case of the Kemper trio, and Wright concluded that anytime "a white lawyer in Mississippi says things are bad and he needs help, then we have to help."[67]

As these deliberations among NAACP officials in New York were occurring, however, the case of the Kemper County trio received a further, devastating blow when John Clark suffered a complete physical and mental collapse. Mrs. Clark reported later that she had realized after the appeal to the Mississippi

Supreme Court that her husband "had reached the breaking point, physically and nervously." "Our physicians tell us that Mr. Clark's illness was caused to a great extent by the work and worry of the fight for the lives of the three negroes," Mrs. Clark said. "He was a sick man when the Judge appointed him to defend the negroes, and for that reason asked to be excused from the case. The Judge insisted on his defending the clients, and when Mr. Clark entered the case he put his whole heart and ability in the defense." "He has been very unjustly criticized and has worried quite a bit because of the lack of help he has had in the hard fight he has waged," she continued. "He has 'fought a good fight and kept the faith.' I have encouraged him and helped in every way possible." "Racial prejudice runs high here," she pointed out, "and the gallows erected for the hanging . . . is a Mecca for people from all over the State. Of course, the justice loving, law abiding people here are in sympathy with Mr. Clark's efforts but many of them dare not express their opinions because of inflamed public sentiment."[68]

John Clark's incapacitation was so severe that well over a year after the decision of the Mississippi Supreme Court affirming the convictions of the Kemper County trio, he was only able to sit up a few hours each day.[69] Ed Brown, Henry Shields, and Yank Ellington had thus lost not only the appeal of their convictions in the state supreme court but also the services of the only attorney who had had the courage to come to their defense after their trial. In their cells in the Lauderdale County jail in Meridian, the Kemper County trio had seen the hopes generated by the appeal to the Mississippi Supreme Court dashed, and the outlook for them appeared gloomy indeed in January 1935.

1. Dan T. Carter, *Scottsboro: A Tragedy of the American South,* rev. ed. (Baton Rouge: Louisiana State University Press, 1979), pp. 11–50, 105–6.

2. Ibid., pp. 51–103.

3. Buchanan v. Warley, 245 U.S. 60 (1917).

4. Guinn v. United States, 238 U.S. 357 (1915); Nixon v. Herndon, 273 U.S. 536 (1927); Nixon v. Condon, 286 U.S. 73 (1932). For a detailed account of the white primary litigation, see Clement E. Vose, *Constitutional Change* (Lexington, Mass.: Lexington Books, 1972), pp. 287–326.

5. Moore v. Dempsey, 261 U.S. 86, 91 (1923).

6. Charles Flint Kellogg, *NAACP: A History of the National Association for the Advancement of Colored People* (Baltimore, Md.: Johns Hopkins University Press, 1967), pp. 241–45.

7. See Powell v. Alabama, 287 U. S. 45 (1932), and Brown v. Mississippi, 297 U.S. 278 (1936).

8. Carter, *Scottsboro*, pp. 51–103.

9. Ibid., p. 138.

10. Ibid., pp. 144–45.

11. Ibid., pp. 96–102.

12. Wilma Dykeman and James Stokely, *Seeds of Southern Change: The Life of Will Alexander* (Chicago: University of Chicago Press, 1962), pp. 5–59, 162.

13. Ibid., p. 78. For an insightful analysis of Alexander's views on the race question, see John B. Kirby, *Black Americans in the Roosevelt Era: Liberalism and Race* (Knoxville: University of Tennessee Press, 1980), pp. 48–62. For a discussion of the CIC's link to the earlier progressive movement in the South, see Dewey W. Grantham, *Southern Progressivism: The Reconciliation of Progress and Tradition* (Knoxville: University of Tennessee Press, 1983), pp. 413–14.

14. Morton Sosna, *In Search of the Silent South: Southern Liberals on the Race Issue* (New York: Columbia University Press, 1977), p. 38.

15. Carter, *Scottsboro*, pp. 123–31.

16. Kirby, *Black Americans in the Roosevelt Era*, p. 54.

17. Carter, *Scottsboro*, pp. 123–31.

18. George B. Tindall, *The Emergence of the New South* (Baton Rouge: Louisiana State University Press, 1967), p. 181; Carter, *Scottsboro*, pp. 108–21, 153–55.

19. Powell v. Alabama, 287 U.S. 45 (1932). The cost of the *Powell* litigation is revealed in a memorandum on the ILD's receipts and expenditures in the case in the ACLU Archives, vol. 646, 31 Dec. 1932. This memorandum indicates that the ILD had spent $14,375.68 for the *Powell* case, running a deficit of $2,820.22.

20. Powell v. Alabama, 287 U.S. 45, 68–69 (1932).

21. Carter, *Scottsboro*, pp. 174–91.

22. Norris v. Alabama, 297 U.S. 587 (1935).

23. Carter, *Scottsboro*, pp. 399–415.

24. Ibid., pp. 235–37. The alternative legal strategy suggested here is therefore similar to that which would be pursued by a tradi-

tional "advocate" rather than that which would be pursued by a member of the "radical bar." On the application of these concepts as they affect litigation strategy, see Jonathan D. Casper, *Lawyers before the Warren Court* (Urbana: University of Illinois Press, 1972). Compare also the strategy suggested here with the factors dictating the effectiveness of NAACP activities in Little Rock, Arkansas, during the 1950s, as noted by Tony Freyer, *The Little Rock Crisis: A Constitutional Interpretation* (Westport, Conn.: Greenwood Press, 1984), pp. 28–29.

25. Carter, *Scottsboro*, p. 393.

26. Mrs. John A. Clark to Arthur Garfield Hays, 12 Dec. 1935, ACLU Archives, vol. 941.

27. Record, *Brown v. Mississippi*, pp. 146–48.

28. Ibid., pp. 146–47.

29. Ibid., p. 148.

30. Ibid., pp. 148–49.

31. Mrs. John A. Clark to Arthur Garfield Hays, 21 Jan. 1936, ACLU Archives, vol. 941.

32. Record, *Brown v. Mississippi*, p. 149.

33. Mrs. John A. Clark to Arthur Garfield Hays, 21 Jan. 1936, ACLU Archives, vol. 941; Jackson *Daily Clarion-Ledger*, 26 Feb. 1940, p. 3; 14 Nov. 1956, p. 6.

34. Mrs. John A. Clark to Arthur Garfield Hays, 21 Jan. 1936, ACLU Archives, vol. 941.

35. Albert D. Kirwan, *The Revolt of the Rednecks: Mississippi Politics: 1876–1925* (Gloucester, Mass.: Peter Smith, 1964), pp. 66–67.

36. See Grantham, *Southern Progressivism*, pp. 36–45. Although it describes Mississippi politics during an earlier period, the description is essentially applicable to Mississippi politics during the 1930s as well.

37. V. O. Key, Jr., *Southern Politics* (New York: Vintage Books, 1949), p. 232; on Vardaman, see also William F. Holmes, *The White Chief: James Kemble Vardaman* (Baton Rouge: Louisiana State University Press, 1970).

38. William Alexander Percy, *Lanterns on the Levee* (New York: Knopf, 1941), p. 148.

39. Kellogg, *NAACP*, p. 233; Robert L. Zangrando, *The NAACP Crusade against Lynching: 1909–1950* (Philadelphia: Temple University Press, 1980), p. 150.

40. Key, *Southern Politics*, p. 242, n. 31; *Life 20 (11 March 1946): 101.*

41. Record, *Brown v. Mississippi*, pp. 125–26, 149; Meridian *Star*, 6 May 1934, p. 1; 8 May 1934, p. 1.

42. *Crisis* 42 (March 1935): 79.

43. Ibid.

44. The jurisdiction of the U.S. Supreme Court, like that of all

federal courts, is limited by Article 3 of the Constitution to cases and controversies arising under the Constitution, laws, and treaties of the United States. For a case to be appealed to the Supreme Court from a state court, therefore, it must be asserted that the case turns on an interpretation of the U.S. Constitution, federal law, or a treaty.

45. Ellis v. State, 65 Miss. 44 (1887).

46. Ibid., p. 48.

47. Loftin v. State, 150 Miss. 228 (1928).

48. Ibid., p. 236–37.

49. Jackson *Daily Clarion-Ledger,* 7 Jan. 1952, p. 1; 8 Jan. 1952, p. 4, editorial, "William Dozier Anderson: Eminent Jurist and Citizen."

50. 150 Miss. 228, 237–38.

51. Brown v. State, 173 Miss. 542 (1935).

52. Ibid., pp. 553–54.

53. Ibid.

54. Ibid., p. 557.

55. Ibid., pp. 557–558.

56. Ibid., pp. 558–60.

57. Ibid., p. 561.

58. Ibid., pp. 561–62.

59. Ibid., pp. 562–63.

60. Ibid., p. 563.

61. Record, *Brown* v. *Mississippi,* p. 137.

62. Meridian *Star,* 7 Jan. 1935, p. 1.

63. Jackson *Daily Clarion-Ledger,* 8 Jan. 1935, p. 16; Jackson *Daily News,* 7 Jan. 1935, pp. 1, 12.

64. Jackson *Daily News,* 6 April 1934, pp. 1, 11.

65. Ibid., 7 Jan. 1935, p. 12.

66. Roy Wilkins, *Standing Fast: The Autobiography of Roy Wilkins* (New York: Viking Press, 1982), p. 141.

67. Ibid., p. 167. Some details in the account of the *Brown* case in Wilkins's autobiography are inaccurate, especially his indication that Thurgood Marshall, counsel for the NAACP, then intervened and took the case to the U.S. Supreme Court. As indicated in Chapter 4 herein, this is an inaccurate portrayal of what occurred after the loss of the first appeal to the Mississippi Supreme Court.

68. Mrs. John A. Clark to Arthur Garfield Hays, 12 Dec. 1935, ACLU Archives, vol. 941.

69. Mrs. John A. Clark to Arthur Garfield Hays, 21 Jan. 1936, ACLU Archives, vol. 941.

4

Earl Brewer's Appeal

Under Mississippi procedure, the only remaining possibility of saving the Kemper County trio from the hangman was the filing of a suggestion of error in the Mississippi Supreme Court. The suggestion of error was in the nature of a petition for a rehearing, a device by which a losing party in a case just decided by the supreme court could request the court to reconsider its decision. As a device to save Ed Brown, Henry Shields, and Yank Ellington from being executed, the suggestion of error was a long shot, since the state supreme court ordinarily dismissed suggestions of error summarily, but the device was the last remaining remedy in the state judicial system for the Kemper trio.

Suggestions of error, however, had to be filed with the Mississippi Supreme Court within fifteen days after the decision which it was being asked to reconsider had been rendered. And with John Clark's physical and mental collapse, it was clear that he was in no condition to prepare a suggestion of error. Recognizing her husband's disability, Mrs. Clark decided that she must act and act quickly. "I went to one of my closest friends," she said later, "Ex-Governor Earl Brewer, who seems almost like a father to me, and begged him to help Mr. Clark in the fight he was making for a humane cause. I told him all the horrible details of the case and he was very indignant and consented to help us solely because of his personal love for Mr. Clark and for the purpose of helping right a grievous wrong." "I told Governor Brewer that he could not count upon a fee," Mrs. Clark continued, "as the negroes were the poorest and most illiterate type of share croppers. Their families could not raise five dollars if all their lives depended upon their so doing."[1]

Ex-Governor Earl Leroy Brewer thus entered the fight to save the lives of the Kemper County trio. Earl Brewer had been born on 11 August 1868, in Carroll County, Mississippi, one of six children born to a Civil War Confederate veteran, Captain Ratliff Rodney Brewer, and his wife, Elizabeth McEachern Brewer. Ratliff Brewer died in 1881, when Earl was thirteen years old, and as the eldest son Earl assumed the responsibility for operating the family farm, which was located on poor soil and was in debt. Brewer early demonstrated unusual capacities, however, since by the time he had turned sixteen, he had paid off the debts on the farm and had made a sufficient profit to operate the farm successfully.[2]

With the marriage of his older sister Eloise, Earl Brewer relinquished the operation of the family farm to his sister's husband and left home for the first time. He worked on a plantation in the Mississippi Delta at Friars Point and subsequently worked on farms and ranches in Texas. While residing in Texarkana, Texas, he also attended a local business school. With the death of his brother-in-law in 1887, Brewer returned home to once again manage the family farm. He entered politics almost immediately, and was elected constable, although at the age of twenty he was unable to vote; later he served as deputy sheriff. At the age of twenty-four, Brewer decided to secure a law degree, but the two-year law course at the University of Mississippi was more than he could financially afford. Upon being advised by the university chancellor to attempt the law course in one year, Brewer borrowed four hundred dollars, entered the law school on 15 November 1891, and graduated in June 1892, six and a half months later.[3]

Establishing a law partnership with a lawschool classmate in Water Valley, Brewer rapidly established himself as a successful attorney. "To be in Heaven in its broadest sense," it was said of him during this period, "Earl Brewer would want vast libraries to work in, midnight oil to burn, crippled clients walking around on crutches, railroad companies to sue and contributory negligence to talk about, etc." One of his clients at this time was Mrs. "Casey" Jones, the widow of the famous railroad engineer killed in a train wreck and heralded in song. After Casey Jones's death, Brewer negotiated an out-of-court settlement with the Illinois Central Railroad Company on behalf of Mrs. Jones.[4]

In 1897, Brewer married Minnie Marian Block of Water Valley, a marriage that produced three daughters, Minnie, Earlene, and Claudia. Brewer's political activities continued, and he was elected to the Mississippi senate in 1895 at the age of twenty-seven, the youngest member of that body. He was reelected to the state senate in 1899 and in 1902 was appointed district attorney for the Eleventh District by Governor Andrew H. Longino, the latter appointment causing Brewer to move his family and law practice to Clarksdale.[5]

In Clarksdale, Brewer formed the kinds of associations common to aspiring politicians. He became an elder in the Presbyterian church, became a Thirty-Third Degree Mason, and was a member of the Odd Fellows, the Elks Club, and the Woodsmen of the World. He resigned as district attorney in 1907 to make his first race for governor at the age of thirty-nine, but he was narrowly beaten in the second Democratic primary by E. F. Noel. In 1911, however, Brewer again ran for governor, and apparently because of his strong showing in the 1907 race, he won the Democratic nomination for governor without opposition. This was the first time in the history of the state that a nomination for governor had gone uncontested.[6]

Theodore G. Bilbo was elected lieutenant governor when Earl Brewer was elected governor, and as a result of a feud between the two, Brewer's administration was a stormy one. As governor, Brewer was determined to root out corruption in state government, and for this purpose hired detectives to investigate various agencies. The result was the exposure of the fact that the state penitentiary board was selling cotton grown by state convicts to a favored company at low prices without competitive bidding. Brewer's detectives also exposed a scandal at the state asylum for the insane at Jackson. Since many of the individuals involved in these scandals were political allies of Lieutenant Governor Bilbo, it became obvious that Brewer's investigations "were the manifestations of a new and bitter rivalry that had sprung up between Brewer and Bilbo."[7] The bitterness between the two was demonstrated when Brewer, pursuing the cotton-selling scandal, traveled to England in September 1915. The malicious rumor soon circulated that Brewer had been accompanied on the trip "by a beautiful inmate of a Memphis brothel," a rumor Brewer charged that Bilbo had originated.[8]

It became the "chief ambition of Governor Brewer's life," it was reported, "to prevent Bilbo being named as his successor."[9] And Brewer appeared to have succeeded in this ambition when Burns detectives he had hired discovered evidence that Bilbo had accepted a bribe to support a bill in the legislature creating a new county. The bribe, it was alleged, was paid by a property owner in the proposed county seat of the new county. Bilbo was indicted in December 1913 and was tried the following June, with Governor Brewer testifying at the trial. When the jury acquitted Bilbo, Brewer expressed his astonishment at the result.[10]

After the trial Bilbo assumed the role of a persecuted martyr. He began his campaign for governor in 1915, with Brewer attempting to rally opposition to him. Brewer urged U.S. Senator James K. Vardaman to oppose Bilbo publicly, but to Brewer's outrage, Vardaman refused to do so. "Senator Vardaman knows as well as I do that Bilbo is a crook," Brewer charged, "but . . . he fears that . . .Bilbo will go right after his position in the Senate." Bilbo, Brewer contended, had committed "numerous frauds and crimes," and was seeking to create a "cabal . . . for securing political advantage for a faction through dirty intrigue." "Never before in the State," he continued, "was political depravity so open and bold and defiant in asserting itself."[11]

Bilbo defeated the candidate for governor backed by Brewer by twenty-five thousand votes, carrying all but three counties in the state. Because of the contempt that Brewer felt toward the new governor, he refused to attend Bilbo's inauguration as his successor. Although Mississippi governors commonly sought election to the U.S. Senate after their terms as governor expired, Earl Brewer retired from politics after Bilbo's election. The editor of the Jackson *Daily News*, who knew Brewer personally, commented on the reasons for his retirement from politics by noting that while "the dominating force of Brewer's personality is tenacity," the ex-governor "was keenly disappointed when he failed to put Bilbo behind the prison bars he felt he deserved."[12] Brewer's only subsequent involvement in elective politics in Mississippi came in 1924, when he attempted to unseat U.S. Senator Pat Harrison but was soundly defeated.[13]

After the unsuccessful battle to keep Theodore Bilbo out of the governor's chair, Earl Brewer returned to his law practice in Clarksdale, where he became involved in large-scale deals in cotton land in the Mississippi Delta. Given the premium prices for Delta cotton at the time, Brewer soon amassed a fortune as a cotton producer. In 1920, however, the bottom dropped out from under cotton prices, and Brewer was caught overextended and was ruined financially. His daughters Minnie and Claudia had been attending the University of Wisconsin, but were forced to leave the university and return home to seek jobs to help the family finances. Brewer himself returned to his law practice and over the next decade slowly rehabilitated his financial condition.[14]

In the winter of 1932–33, Brewer defended a long time friend who was commissioner of the state tax office in a case tried in Jackson, the state capital. Brewer's brilliant performance in that case, at the age of sixty-four, drew the attention of the state press and proved to be the turning point in his struggle to overcome his financial ruin in 1920. Brewer's performance at the trial, the Jackson *Daily News* commented in an editorial titled "Earl Brewer's Comeback," proved "conclusively that he has lost none of his skill as a criminal lawyer. His generalship in handling the case was masterly, and from the beginning spectators in the courtroom had little doubt about how the case would end." A quarter of a century earlier, the *News* noted, Brewer had had "a head covered with curly raven locks. Today his hair is somewhat thin and white as driven snow, but in the memorable battle [at the trial], it became quite evident that he is not using his head merely as a loafing place on which to hang a hat."[15]

His success at the trial in Jackson led Brewer to transfer his residence and law practice from Clarksdale to Jackson, and it was there that Mrs. Clark begged him to undertake the defense of the Kemper County trio in the winter of 1935. With his agreement to undertake the defense, the Kemper trio gained as their defender a wily veteran of Mississippi political and legal battles as well as a man who bore the scars of personal misfortune. And they also gained a lawyer who would save their lives.[16]

Earl Brewer's first problem in defending the Kemper trio was the fact that the fifteen-day deadline for filing suggestions of error with the Mississippi Supreme Court had expired by the time he entered the case. Brewer petitioned the supreme court for an extension of the deadline, and the court granted him an additional fifteen days to file the suggestion of error. Working rapidly under the pressure of the new deadline, Brewer finally filed the suggestion of error with the court on 5 February 1935. Since the Kemper trio were scheduled to be hanged on 8 February, Brewer also requested that Governor Sennett Conner grant a reprieve postponing the executions, and on 2 February Conner granted the request, postponing the executions until 21 February. By only the barest of margins, Brown, Shields, and Ellington thus missed being hanged in the winter of 1935.[17]

A rumor circulated in DeKalb and Meridian that if the Mississippi Supreme Court rejected Brewer's suggestion of error, there would be an appeal to the U.S. Supreme Court, and this created another threat to the lives of the Kemper trio. "All three condemned men are in the county jail at Meridian," the Jackson *Daily News* reported, "but when an appeal to the federal courts was rumored, feeling in DeKalb and in Meridian ran so high that plans were made to transfer them to Jackson in an emergency."[18] Fearing that a lynch mob might attack the jail in Meridian, on 3 February Lauderdale County sheriff B. M. Stephens ordered two of his deputies to escort Brown, Shields, and Ellington to the "mob-proof" Hinds County jail in Jackson.[19]

The Hinds County jail sat atop the million-dollar Hinds County courthouse in Jackson, and it was a common practice for sheriffs in outlying counties to transfer convicted murderers to Jackson. "It has become quite the custom with sheriffs all over the state," the Jackson *Daily News* complained editorially, "when they have a condemned murderer on hand to rush him to the escape-proof jail in Jackson for safe-keeping. This is done even in instances when the condemned men are not regarded as especially desperate or where there is no imminent danger of mob violence." Indeed, other prisoners at the Hinds County jail complained about being housed with so many murderers.[20] "Death hovers over the Hinds County jail at Jackson—a horrible death, dangling, swaying, twisting at the end of a rope," the *Daily News* reported on February 5. "The Mississippi 'Scottsboro case' principals," Brown, Shields, and Ellington, the *Daily News* continued, "sit in stolid silence."[21]

A month after the transfer of the Kemper trio to Jackson, the press reported that Yank Ellington was "in such a condition he may not live to hear the decision of the supreme court on a suggestion of error."[22] The Hinds County physician said that Ellington "will die in a few days unless given proper hospital care," and Hinds County sheriff John Roberts telephoned Kemper County sheriff J. D. Adcock to advise him of Ellington's condition and the county physician's recommendation. Since Ellington was being held under the authority of the Kemper County circuit court, permission of Kemper County officials was required to move him to a hospital, but Kemper County officials refused to give their permission. Kemper County sheriff Adcock said that "Kemper County would furnish medicine and doctor's services for the negro in the jail here," the Jackson *Daily News* reported, "but would not authorize his transfer to a hospital. Should he be moved Sheriff Adcock said he would have to be guarded day and night as a desperate character even in the hospital and Kemper county would not stand the expense of a guard."[23]

Hinds County sheriff Roberts said "he and his staff are

doing everything possible to make the negro comfortable," the *Daily News* reported. Ellington complained of continual chest pains "where he claims he was 'stomped' when a mob allegedly beat him up to obtain the confession on which he and the other two were convicted—the method of obtaining the confession being the basis of an appeal now before the Supreme Court on suggestion of error."[24] Despite being denied hospital care, Ellington fortunately was reported to be recovering from his injuries by early May.[25]

Matters were improving for the Kemper County trio on other fronts as well. Although the National Association for the Advancement of Colored People had contributed only a nominal sum to the trio's case as John Clark appealed it to the state supreme court, the association pledged its full financial support to Earl Brewer and agreed to pay for an appeal to the U.S. Supreme Court, if necessary. The association announced in March 1935 that "three Mississippi cotton field workers who probably never heard of the National Association for the Advancement of Colored People are alive today with a fighting chance for freedom because of the existence of the N.A.A.C.P." The NAACP praised John Clark's efforts on behalf of the Kemper trio, pointing out that Clark, unlike the other court-appointed lawyers at the trial, "did not shirk the task," but rather had appealed the case to the Mississippi Supreme Court. "All this action took place," the association admitted, "without the assistance of any organization, or, indeed, of any colored people in or near Kemper County."[26]

When Clark contacted the association's national office for aid in the appeal, the NAACP said, the "national office, having practically no legal defense funds, sent a small check last July as a contribution and awaited the decision of the supreme court." The basis "for the intervention of the association" after the Supreme Court had affirmed the convictions of the Kemper trio, the NAACP noted, "was furnished by Judge W. D. Anderson of the state supreme court who refused to join his associates in affirming the death sentences of the lower court, and who wrote a strong dissenting opinion saying the only evidence against the men had been secured by torture and that the defendants had not had a fair trial." The association noted that the case was pending a rehearing before the Mississippi Supreme Court and that it had "pledged itself to raise the money to carry the appeal to the United States Supreme Court."[27]

The NAACP criticized the black community in Mississippi for its failure to rise to the defense of Brown, Shields, and Ellington. "Meridian, Miss., is only forty miles south of De-Kalb, but the colored people of Meridian kept silent," the NAACP pointed out. "The story of what Judge Anderson describes as 'brutal whippings and beatings' failed to stir them to action." "Mississippi," the association noted, "is the one state that so far has been unorganized by the association. Her colored citizens seem afraid to lift their voices or pool their money to fight for themselves."[28]

Because it was short of funds, the NAACP issued a nation-wide appeal for contributions to support the litigation in the Kemper County trio case. In April, the association printed a picture of Brown, Shields, and Ellington on the front cover of the *Crisis,* the NAACP's monthly publication, and appealed for funds. In the picture of the trio, the association pointed out, "Ellington, in the center, is being held up by his two companions. That is because he is nearly dead from the torture he received when a 'confession' was forced out of him. He was beaten and hanged a little at a time to make him confess. As a result his neck is damaged and he is injured so severely otherwise that he cannot sit up alone." "Ellington," the NAACP continued, "is likely to die in jail before final legal action on his appeal can be taken." "Funds are badly needed by the national office for this and other legal cases pending," the association concluded. "Practically all funds for this case must be raised outside of Mississippi."[29]

Although the NAACP criticized the Mississippi black community for its failure to come to the defense of the Kemper trio, James A. Burns, a black attorney in Mississippi, had been in communication with Roy Wilkins of the NAACP concerning the case. And when the association decided to intervene on behalf of the trio, Burns expressed his delight to Wilkins. "Your letter relative to the Kemper race men and the action by the NAACP in their case brings joy truly to me," Burns wrote Wilkins. "To say that I am glad is only putting it mildly. For I have been certainly worried about the apathy which has been exhibited by my people in this locality over their case."[30]

Burns complained, however, because the NAACP had retained Earl Brewer, a white lawyer, to represent the trio. "The only thing that I regret is that the organization has seen fit to employ white lawyers in the matter exclusively," Burns told Wilkins. "You cannot imagine what harm that has done to the standing of colored lawyers in the estimation of our race in this part of the country. At this time, there are just *five* colored lawyers in this entire state engaged in the active practice of law, and we are almost without clientele among our people because they are saying that we can do them no good before the courts." "However," Burns concluded, "that is a matter that I can take up with your organization after this matter is concluded."[31]

The NAACP's criticism of the Mississippi black community also stirred the consciences of the blacks in Meridian, with the result that they organized a branch of the NAACP. Roy L. Young, president of the Meridian NAACP branch, wrote Roy Wilkins in March 1935 that the article criticizing Mississippi blacks published in the *Crisis* "has meant much in molding sentiment. Our people have decided to take a stand, whatever the cost may be." "You hit us such a blow in this month's Crisis," Young continued, "all of which seemed to have been true, that we MUST show and prove to you that we mean business."[32]

By the end of March, the NAACP announced that a branch of the association had been organized in Meridian with 126 charter members. "This is the first active unit of the N.A.A.C.P. in the state of Mississippi in many years," the association announced. "There are skeleton organizations in Panola County and Jackson. Meridian citizens were spurred to act by the case arising in Kemper county where Ed Brown, Henry Shields and Yank Ellington were brutally beaten and 'forced to confess' to the murder of a white planter."[33] The NAACP's branch in Jackson also became active once again because of the Kemper County trio's case.[34]

Although the NAACP as well as local Mississippi blacks had at last entered the fight to save Brown, Shields, and Ellington, and the association had pledged to finance an appeal to the U.S. Supreme Court, it was up to Earl Brewer to lay the basis for a Supreme Court appeal if that became necessary. John Clark had failed to allege in the first appeal of the case to the Mississippi Supreme Court that any violations of the federal Constitution had occurred in the proceedings against the Kemper trio, and it was up to Earl Brewer to correct that error and to raise federal constitutional questions in the suggestion of error so that there would be a basis for an appeal to the U.S. Supreme Court should that step have to be taken.

In the suggestion of error, Brewer therefore alleged for the first time that the proceedings against the Kemper trio had violated the Due Process Clause of the Fourteenth Amendment, as well as Mississippi law. To a great extent, the suggestion of error tracked the points made in Judge William D. Anderson's dissenting opinion from the Mississippi Supreme Court's first decision affirming the convictions. In the hearing at the trial on the admissibility of the confessions of the Kemper trio, Earl Brewer argued, the testimony of Kemper County sheriff Adcock had revealed sufficient facts to demonstrate that the defendants' confessions had not been freely and voluntarily made. Judge Sturdivant's ruling allowing testimony regarding the confessions to be heard by the jury, Brewer therefore asserted, had denied Brown, Shields, and Ellington not only their rights under the constitution and laws of Mississippi, which required confessions to be free and voluntary in order to be admissible in criminal trials, but also denied the trio "due process of law, within the meaning of the Fourteenth Amendment of the Federal Constitution."[35]

After the defendants had testified that their confessions had been coerced, Brewer also contended, and after rebuttal witnesses called by the prosecution confirmed the defendants' testimony, the trial court "on its own motion" should have excluded the confessions of the defendants. The failure of the trial court to exclude the confessions after testimony had shown them to be the result of force and violence against the defendants "amounted to a denial of a fair and impartial trial, as guaranteed by the Constitution of the State of Mississippi; and

to a denial of due process of law, as guaranteed by the Fourteenth Amendment to the Federal Constitution."[36]

Earl Brewer therefore attempted in his suggestion of error
to correct John Clark's mistake in not raising federal constitutional issues in Clark's appeal of the Kemper trio's case to the
Mississippi Supreme Court. In arguing that the use of coerced
confessions as evidence against Brown, Shields, and Ellington
was reversible error, Brewer invoked the Due Process Clause of
the Fourteenth Amendment and its guarantee of a fair trial in
state criminal proceedings. In attacking the use of the coerced
confessions, Brewer could not invoke the Self-Incrimination
Clause of the Fifth Amendment of the federal Constitution,
since the U.S. Supreme Court had held in 1908 in *Twining* v.
New Jersey that the Self-Incrimination Clause of the Fifth
Amendment applied only in federal trials and proceedings and
not in state proceedings.[37] Section 26 of the Mississippi Constitution also prohibited compulsory self-incrimination, however, and Brewer argued in his suggestion of error that the use
of coerced confessions as evidence against criminal defendants
violated Section 26 of the state constitution.[38]

Brewer further bolstered his argument that the use of
coerced confessions in a state criminal proceeding denied the
right to a fair trial by invoking the U.S. Supreme Court's
decision in *Mooney* v. *Holohan,* a case decided by the Court
approximately a month prior to the filing of Brewer's suggestion of error.[39] In the *Mooney* case, the Supreme Court held
that the knowing use of perjured testimony by the prosecution
in a criminal trial denied the defendant a fair trial within the
meaning of the Due Process Clause of the Fourteenth Amendment, and Earl Brewer contended in the suggestion of error
that the knowing use of confessions procured by torture by the
prosecution was condemned by the principle of the *Mooney*
case. When a prosecutor used either perjured testimony or a
coerced confession, Brewer argued, the prosecutor was knowingly using false evidence to convict a defendant in violation of
the due process right to a fair trial, since, analytically, there
was no essential difference between perjured testimony and a
coerced confession.[40]

Brewer finally contended in the suggestion of error that the convictions of Brown, Shields, and Ellington had also violated the Due Process Clause of the Fourteenth Amendment because they had been denied the effective assistance of counsel at their trial in violation of the principles laid down by the U.S. Supreme Court in the Scottsboro case, *Powell* v. *Alabama.* There had been inadequate time for defense counsel to consult with their clients prior to the Kemper trio's trial, he argued, and some of the defense attorneys had believed their clients were guilty and had therefore offered only an anemic defense at the trial.[41]

On the day after the trial of Brown, Shields, and Ellington, Judge Sturdivant had signed the minutes of the trial and had adjourned the term of the court, thus effectively preventing the filing of a motion for a new trial, since such motions were required to be filed during the term of the court in which the trial being challenged in such a motion had occurred. Because a motion for a new trial had been precluded by Judge Sturdivant's action, Earl Brewer decided to file in the Mississippi Supreme Court a motion in arrest of judgment and for a new trial, in addition to the suggestion of error. In the motion in arrest of judgment and for a new trial, Brewer detailed the torture to which the Kemper trio had been subjected, and he argued that "all the evidence of alleged guilt shown against them was brought about by threat, coercion and brutality and because this was known to the Court and District Attorney when they were convicted in the lower court, and . . .this coercion and threats [were] continued and carried on up to and through their trial," Brown, Shields, and Ellington could not possibly have received a fair trial within the meaning of due process of law.[42]

The primary thrust of the motion in arrest of judgment and for a new trial, however, was to emphasize the right-to-counsel issue under the principles of *Powell* v. *Alabama.* The Kemper County trio had been denied the effective assistance of counsel at their trial as required by the *Powell* case, Brewer argued in the motion, since "they were denied [the] opportunity to confer with their counsel in an orderly and reasonable manner and . . .they were denied any opportunity to make a motion for a new trial and . . .this trial amounted to depriving them of their life without due process of law under the Constitution of the United States." The trial the three blacks had received, Brewer contended, was not the kind of trial required either by the constitution and laws of Mississippi or by the U. S. Constitution but rather violated both.[43]

Attached to the motion in arrest of judgment and for a new trial were sworn affidavits by John Clark, Ed Brown, Henry Shields, and Yank Ellington. In his affidavit, Clark detailed the haste with which the trial had been conducted and the inadequacy of the defense the defense attorneys, including himself, had offered for the Kemper trio at their trial.[44] And the three blacks described in their affidavits the torture to which they had been subjected to secure false confessions from them. Each also confirmed the allegations in Clark's affidavit that they had been inadequately defended at their trial and concluded by swearing that they were innocent of killing Raymond Stuart.[45]

The points raised in the suggestion of error and in the motion for a new trial were argued orally by Earl Brewer and counsel for the state before the Mississippi Supreme Court on 7 February 1935.[46] Although the state supreme court normally dismissed suggestions of error summarily, Earl Brewer's arguments on behalf of the Kemper trio apparently made an impression with the court, since two weeks after the oral argument, the court ordered the state attorney general's office to file a brief in the case by 28 February, while Brewer was ordered to file a reply brief five days later. Although Governor Conner's stay of execution would expire on 21 February, the press pointed out that since the state supreme court had retained jurisdiction in the case, the execution of the Kemper trio would be indefinitely postponed until the court had rendered a final disposition of the case. The action of the supreme court in ordering briefs, the press also noted, "is an unusual, but not exceptional procedure. . . . Ordinarily the court hears suggestions of error and overrules them with little to do."[47]

The result of the Mississippi Supreme Court's thorough consideration of the second appeal was that a decision in the case of the Kemper county trio was delayed until 29 April 1935.

When the decision was announced, however, the court once again sustained the validity of the convictions of Brown, Shields, and Ellington. The court again reaffirmed its adherence to the rule of *Loftin* v. *State* that a confession, even if shown to be coerced, was admissible as evidence in Mississippi courts in the absence of a timely objection by defense counsel to its admission. The trial court, the supreme court again held, had properly ruled the confessions of Brown, Shields, and Ellington to be admissible on the basis of the testimony presented in the hearing in the absence of the jury, and after testimony was presented indicating that the confessions were in fact coerced, no "request was there or thereafter made that the confessions be excluded as evidence." In the absence of such a request by defense counsel, the court again ruled, the trial court "was under no duty to exclude the confessions and therefore could not be held to have erred in not so doing." "We must decline to overrule Loftin's case," the supreme court said, "and apply here a rule different from the rule applied there."[48]

Earl Brewer had argued, the court noted, that the admission of coerced confessions as evidence in a criminal trial constituted a violation of Section 26 of the Mississippi Constitution, which prohibited compulsory self-incrimination. The court conceded that it assumed that Brewer's contention on this point was correct, but it pointed out that if the prohibition against self-incrimination protected by the state constitution was to be invoked against a coerced confession, the defendant or his counsel must specifically invoke the right during the trial, for otherwise the right would be considered to have been waived. And this was precisely what had occurred at the trial of the Kemper trio, the supreme court continued, since "the record discloses no objection to the confessions on the ground of self-incrimination, but aside from that, they were competent when admitted, and, although the . . . [Kemper trio] had the right and opportunity so to do, no request to exclude them was made after evidence tending to show their incompetency was introduced."[49]

The supreme court next addressed the question whether the due process provisions of the state constitution as well as the Due Process Clause of the Fourteenth Amendment of the

U.S. Constitution had been violated by the proceedings against the Kemper County trio. The right against compulsory self-incrimination, the court noted, had been held by the U.S. Supreme Court in *Twining* v. *New Jersey* not to be essential to due process of law, and therefore a claim that the right against compulsory self-incrimination had been violated could not be used to assert that there had been a denial of due process of law either under the state constitution or the federal Constitution. Due process, as guaranteed by both the state and federal constitutions, the court pointed out, merely guaranteed to criminal defendants the right to a fair trial according to the traditional modes of proceeding. The procedure at the trial of the Kemper trio, the court continued, "was in accord with that applicable to all civil and criminal trials, recognized in all common law jurisdictions, and did not result in arbitrarily depriving the . . . [trio] of any constitutional or common law right. This is all that the due process clauses of the two constitutions require. The authorities in support thereof are so numerous as to make their citation supererogatory."[50]

Earl Brewer's argument, based on *Mooney* v. *Holohan*, that the use of a coerced confession as evidence in a trial was essentially the same as the use of perjured testimony, was also rejected by the supreme court. In the *Mooney* case, the court pointed out, the charge was that Mooney had been convicted on the basis of evidence known to be perjury by the prosecutor and that the prosecutor had nevertheless concealed that fact from defense counsel and the defendant Mooney. In the case of the Kemper trio, there had been no perjury or suppression of evidence favorable to the defense by the prosecution, the court said, and all the facts related to the confessions of the defendants being coerced were known both by the defendants and their counsel at the trial. The principle of the *Mooney* case, the court thus ruled, was inapplicable to the case before it.[51]

The court acknowledged that Earl Brewer had filed a motion in arrest of judgment and for a new trial in addition to the suggestion of error, but it refused to consider this motion or the affidavits of John Clark and Brown, Shields, and Ellington attached to the motion. The place to file a motion in arrest of judgment or for a new trial was in the trial court, the court held, and such motions would not "lie in the supreme court." "The supreme court reviews only the rulings of the court below complained of in an assignment of error," the court continued, "and in so doing is confined to an examination of the record made in the court below. It is not a court of original jurisdiction, but of appellate jurisdiction only, and therefore we cannot here examine or consider the allegations in the motion for arrest of judgment, nor the affidavits filed in support thereof."[52]

Although the supreme court therefore refused to consider the motion in arrest of judgment and for a new trial in which Earl Brewer had made his most extensive argument regarding the right to counsel as established in *Powell* v. *Alabama,* the court nevertheless addressed the right-to-counsel issue in its opinion. The court acknowledged that Brewer, in arguing that the Kemper trio had been denied the effective assistance of counsel at the trial, had declared that the three blacks had consequently "stood before the trial court as helpless to defend themselves as sheep in a slaughter pen." In justice to the trial court, the supreme court said, "we must say that this charge is not even remotely supported by the record. It is based probably on things stated in ex parte affidavits in support of the motion in arrest of judgment which have no place in this discussion."[53]

Brewer had also argued that "surely it is cruel folly for the State to contend, in a court of justice, that these negroes are to be bound by the strictest and most technical rules of practice and pleading—and this after their right to counsel has been effectively denied." But the supreme court pointed out that counsel for the Kemper trio had not asked the trial court to continue the case or grant additional time for the preparation of the case for the defense. "The attorneys who defended the . . . [Kemper trio] in the court below are able lawyers of extensive practice—veterans of many forensic conflicts," the court said, "and the record does not disclose that they consciously failed to discharge any duty they owed the . . . [Kemper trio]."[54]

"The rules of procedure here applied are technical only in the sense that all such rules are, and what the . . . [defendants] request is simply that they be excepted from the procedures heretofore uniformly applied to all litigants," the court continued. "This we cannot do." In conclusion, however, the court indicated a certain defensiveness regarding its second affirmation of the convictions of Brown, Shields, and Ellington. "All litigants, of every race and color, are equal at the bar of this court, and we would feel deeply humiliated if the contrary could be justly said," the court concluded. "Nothing herein said is intended to even remotely sanction the method by which these confessions were obtained."[55]

Although Judge William D. Anderson had dissented alone from the Mississippi Supreme Court's decision of the Kemper trio's first appeal, the court divided four to two in the decision of the second appeal, with Judge Virgil Alexis Griffith writing a bitingly eloquent dissent joined by Judge Anderson. Virgil Griffith, born in Silver City, in Lawrence County, and educated at the University of Mississippi, had been admitted to the bar in 1898. He practiced law at Gulfport and was elected to the Eighth District chancery court in 1920. Griffith's campaign for a position on the supreme court in 1928 sparked some controversy because his candidacy was openly supported by Governor Theodore Bilbo, but he nonetheless defeated an incumbent supreme court judge in the election and took his seat on the court in January 1929.[56]

In his dissenting opinion, Judge Griffith pointed out that the record disclosed that Yank Ellington had been seized by a mob and "they hanged him by a rope to the limb of a tree, and having let him down they hung him again, and when he was let down the second time, and he still protested his innocence, he was tied to a tree and whipped, and still declining to accede to the demands that he confess, he was finally released and he returned with some difficulty to his home suffering intense pain and agony." Ellington was subsequently arrested by Deputy Sheriff Dial, Griffith noted, who "severely whipped the defendant, declaring that he would continue the whipping until he confessed, and the defendant then agreed to confess to such a statement as the deputy would dictate, and he did so, after which he was delivered to jail."[57]

Ed Brown and Henry Shields, Griffith continued, had

been subjected to similar treatment at the Meridian jail, where they "were made to strip and they were laid over chairs and their backs were cut to pieces with a leather strap with buckles on it, and they were likewise made by the said deputy definitely to understand that the whipping would be continued unless and until they confessed, and not only confessed, but confessed in every matter of detail as demanded by those present; and in this manner the defendants confessed the crime, and as the whippings progressed and were repeated they changed or adjusted their confession in all particulars of detail so as to conform to the demands of their torturers."[58]

"Further details of the brutal treatment to which these helpless prisoners were subjected need not be pursued," Griffith declared. "It is sufficient to say that in pertinent respects the transcript reads more like pages torn from some medieval account, than a record made within the confines of a modern civilization which aspires to an enlightened constitutional government."[59]

After the confessions had been secured by torture, the sheriffs of Kemper and Lauderdale counties were then summoned to hear "the free and voluntary confessions of these miserable and abject defendants," Griffith sarcastically pointed out. And even though Henry Shields stated that he could not sit down because of the severity of the beating he had undergone, and though Yank Ellington's neck clearly had rope burns on it, he continued, "the solemn farce" of hearing the defendants' confessions was gone through as if they had been free and voluntary.[60]

As Judge Anderson had maintained in his dissent in the first appeal, Griffith contended that Judge Sturdivant should have excluded the confessions at the outset of the trial because they clearly were not free and voluntary beyond a reasonable doubt. And this failure of Judge Sturdivant to exclude the confessions was reversible error, he argued, "under every rule of procedure that has heretofore been prescribed," and it was therefore unnecessary for defense counsel to move the exclusion of the confessions subsequently during the trial.[61]

Without the confessions of the defendants as evidence in the case, Griffith continued, "a peremptory instruction to find for the defendants would have been inescapable," and that the confessions of the Kemper trio had been coerced was uncontradicted by any of the testimony at the trial. Even Deputy Sheriff Cliff Dial admitted the beatings, he pointed out, and "in his testimony with reference to the whipping of defendant Ellington, and in response to the inquiry as to how severely he was whipped, the deputy stated, 'not too much for a negro; not as much as I would have done if it were left to me.'" Two other prosecution witnesses also admitted that Brown, Shields, and Ellington had been whipped, and indeed "not a single witness was introduced who denied it," Griffith declared. "The facts are not only undisputed, they are admitted—and admitted to have been done by officers of the state, in conjunction with other participants, and all this was definitely well known to everybody connected with the trial, and during the trial, including the State's prosecuting attorney and the trial judge presiding."[62]

In addition to being convicted upon the basis of coerced confessions, Griffith added, the Kemper trio had also been denied the effective assistance of counsel at their trial, in violation of the principles announced by the U.S. Supreme Court in the Scottsboro case, *Powell* v. *Alabama*. The counsel for the defense, he argued, had been hurried to trial without proper preparation, and as a result they had not objected to the use of the confessions of the Kemper trio as evidence at the proper time during the trial. On that ground, he continued, the majority of the court had seized upon *Loftin* v. *State* "as a means of sanctioning the appalling violation of fundamental constitutional rights openly disclosed by this record, undisputed and admitted."[63]

For the majority of the supreme court to hold that the confessions of the Kemper trio had been validly considered in the trial court because defense counsel failed to object to their admissibility, Griffith declared, was essentially the same as a ruling that "a lynching party has become legitimate and legal because the victim, while being hung by a mob, did not object in the proper form of words at precisely the proper stage of the proceedings. In my judgment there is no proper form of words, not any proper stage of the proceedings in any such case as the record of the so-called trial now before us disclosed; it was never a legitimate proceeding from beginning to end—it was never anything but a factitious continuation of the mob which originally instituted and engaged in the admitted tortures."[64]

At this point in his dissenting opinion, Judge Griffith rather explicitly invited the U.S. Supreme Court to reverse the decision of his colleagues, assuming that an appeal to the Court were made. "If this judgment be affirmed by the Federal Supreme Court," he said, "it will be first in the history of that court wherein there was allowed to stand a conviction based solely upon testimony coerced by the barbarities of executive officers of the state, known to the prosecuting officers of the state as having been so coerced, when the testimony was introduced, and fully shown in all its nakedness to the trial judge before he closed the case and submitted it to the jury, and when all this is not only undisputed, but is expressly and openly admitted." "The Scottsboro cases," Griffith pointedly added, "are models of correct constitutional procedure as compared with this now before the court. In fundamental respects, it is no better than the case reviewed in Moore v. Dempsey," in which the U.S. Supreme Court had held that a trial dominated by a mob violated the Due Process Clause of the Fourteenth Amendment.[65]

"It may be that in a rarely occasional case which arouses the flaming indignation of a whole community, as was the case here, we shall continue yet for a long time to have outbreaks of the mob or resorts to its methods," Judge Griffith concluded. "But if mobs and mob methods must be, it would be better that their existence and their methods shall be kept wholly separate from the courts; that there shall be no blending of the devices of the mob and the proceedings of the courts; that what the mob has so nearly completed let them finish, and that no court shall by adoption give legitimacy to any of the works of the mob, nor cover by the frills and furbelows of a pretended legal trial the body of that which in fact is the product of the mob, and then, by closing the eyes to actualities, complacently adjudicate that the law of the land has been observed and preserved."[66]

The Mississippi Supreme Court set 6 June 1935 as the new date on which Brown, Shields, and Ellington were to be executed,[67] but the powerful and eloquent dissenting opinion by Judge Griffith, and some of the language even in the majority opinion, created serious doubts that the death sentences would ever be carried out. For even the majority of the Mississippi Supreme Court had declared in the conclusion of its opinion that nothing it had said should "even remotely sanction the method by which these confessions were obtained," and throughout the entire history of the proceedings against the Kemper County trio, no more scathing or eloquent condemnation of the treatment to which they had been subjected by Mississippi officials would surpass the dissenting opinion of Judge Griffith. With Judge William Anderson joining Griffith's dissent, two judges of Mississippi's highest court had not only denounced the proceedings against Brown, Shields, and Ellington in the sharpest possible terms but had also openly declared their belief that the Kemper trio's convictions should be reversed by the U.S. Supreme Court. As with Judge Anderson's dissent in the first appeal, this was of incalculable benefit to the defense efforts.

The powerful dissent of Judge Griffith was extensively quoted in press reports of the supreme court's decision, and the press acknowledged without criticism that the issues in the case of the Kemper County trio would ultimately be presented on appeal to the U.S. Supreme Court. "Affirm Death for 3 Negroes" was the headline in the Meridian *Star's* report of the state supreme court's decision, but the *Star* noted that the court was "sharply divided" and that even the majority of the court had agreed that "the 'tortuous' methods used in obtaining confessions were not 'to be condoned or even remotely sanctioned.'" The court's decision, the *Star* said "paved the way for an appeal of the case to the United States Supreme Court."[68] And although the Jackson *Daily News* pointed out that the murder of Raymond Stuart was "one of the most fiendish crimes in current state history," it also reported that "counsel for the defendants indicated they will take an immediate appeal to [the] federal courts."[69] The Jackson *Daily Clarion-Ledger* similarly acknowledged that the state supreme court's decision would not be the end of the Kemper trio's case. "While no formal appeal has been made to the governor to save the three negroes from the gallows," the *Clarion-Ledger* reported, "it is regarded as almost certain that this will be the next step in the case. Attorneys for the trio are expected either to ask the governor for clemency or attempt to get the case before the supreme court of the United States."[70]

Although the second appeal to the Mississippi Supreme Court had not succeeded in winning a reversal of the Kemper trio's convictions, the prospects for Ed Brown, Henry Shields, and Yank Ellington were brighter in the spring of 1935 than at any time since their trial a year previously. The defense efforts were now led by Earl Brewer, who was a respected figure in Mississippi and well connected politically as an ex-governor and elder statesman. The rightness of the defense's cause had been eloquently endorsed by two judges of the state supreme court, conferring additional respectability and legitimacy upon the defense efforts, and the press appeared to accept the inevitability of an appeal to the U.S. Supreme Court without rancor. As a result of the second appeal to the Mississippi Supreme Court, Earl Brewer had also been able to raise federal constitutional questions under the Due Process Clause of the Fourteenth Amendment, thus correcting John Clark's mistake in that regard in the first appeal and laying the basis for an appeal to the U.S. Supreme Court. The NAACP had in addition pledged its support for the defense of the Kemper County trio, but most importantly, the fact that the NAACP had intervened in the case had not been publicized in Mississippi, and, indeed, the NAACP's role in the litigation was never mentioned in the state's press. The defense had therefore succeeded in avoiding the stigma that would have attached to being publicly identified as affiliated with an "outside," Northern group interfering in Mississippi affairs.

The next step was the filing of a petition for a writ of certiorari with the U.S. Supreme Court with the hope that the Court would agree to review *Brown* v. *Mississippi*— as the case of the Kemper trio would now be styled—and reverse the convictions.

1. Mrs. John A. Clark to Arthur Garfield Hays, 21 January 1936, ACLU Archives, vol. 941.

2. Martha Harrison Williford and Claudia Brewer Strite, "Biography of Earl Leroy Brewer" (unpublished ms.), pp. 1–3. I express my appreciation to Mrs. Claudia Brewer Strite for furnishing me with this unpublished biography of her father.

3. Ibid., pp. 3–4.

4. Ibid., pp. 5–8.

5. Ibid., pp. 5–8.

6. Ibid., p. 9; Albert D. Kirwan, *Revolt of the Rednecks: Mississippi Politics: 1876–1925* (Gloucester, Mass.: Peter Smith, 1964), p. 230.

7. Kirwan, *Revolt of the Rednecks*, p. 239.

8. A. Wigfall Green, *The Man Bilbo* (Baton Rouge: Louisiana State University Press, 1963), p. 45.

9. Green, *The Man Bilbo*, p. 50.

10. Kirwan, *Revolt of the Rednecks*, pp. 242–50.

11. Ibid., pp. 253–55.

12. Williford and Strite, "Biography", pp. 15–16; Kirwan, *Revolt of the Rednecks*, p. 257.

13. Williford and Strite, "Biography," p. 22; Kirwan, *Revolt of the Rednecks*, pp. 305–6.

14. Williford and Strite, "Biography," pp. 20–22.

15. Ibid., p. 39.

16. Ibid., pp. 22–23.

17. Record, *Brown* v. *Mississippi*, pp. 138–39; Jackson *Daily News*, 31, Jan. 1935, p. 1; 3 Feb. 1931, p. 1.

18. Jackson *Daily News*, 3 Feb. 1935, p. 1.

19. Meridian *Star*, 4 Feb. 1935, p. 12.

20. Jackson *Daily News*, 3 March 1935, p. 6, editorial, "Don't Like Murderers."

21. Ibid., 5 Feb. 1935, pp. 1–8.

22. Meridian *Star* 4 March 1935, p. 1.

23. Jackson *Daily News*, 4 March 1935, pp. 1, 8.

24. Ibid., pp. 1, 8.

25. Ibid., 7 May 1935, pp. 11–12.

26. *Crisis* 42 (March 1935): 79.

27. Ibid.

28. Ibid.

29. Ibid., 42 (April 1935): 119.

30. James A. Burns to Roy Wilkins, 6 Feb. 1935, NAACP Papers, G–106.

31. Ibid.

32. Roy L. Young to Roy Wilkins, 12 March 1935, NAACP Papers, G–106.

33. NAACP news release, 29 March 1935, NAACP Papers, G–106; *Crisis* 42 (May 1935): 152.

34. A. W. Wells to NAACP, 13 May 1935, NAACP Papers, G–105.

35. Suggestion of Error, 6 Feb. 1935, record, *Brown v. Mississippi*, pp. 138–39.

36. Ibid, p. 139.

37. Twining v. New Jersey, 211 U.S. 78 (1908).

38. Brown v. State, 173 Miss. 563, 566–67 (1935).

39. Mooney v. Holohan, 297 U.S. 103 (1935).

40. Record, *Brown v. Mississippi*, pp. 139–40.

41. Ibid., p. 140.

42. Ibid., p. 141.

43. Ibid., pp. 142–45.

44. Ibid., pp. 146–47.

45. Ibid., pp. 149–61.

46. Jackson *Daily News*, 7 Feb. 1935, p. 1.

47. Ibid., 17 Feb. 1935, p. 11.

48. Brown v. State, 173 Miss. 563, 564–65 (1935)

49. Ibid., pp. 566–67.

50. Ibid., pp. 567–68.

51. Ibid., pp. 568–69.

52. Ibid., p. 571.

53. Ibid.

54. Ibid., pp 571–72.

55. Ibid., p. 572.

56. Jackson *Daily Clarion-Ledger*, 9 Sept. 1928, p. 4; 11 Sept. 1928, p. 9; 8 Jan. 1929, p. 11; 6 Oct. 1953, p. 1; 8 Oct. 1953, p. 16, editorial, "Judge Griffith Made Many Fine Contributions."

57. Brown v. State, 173 Miss. 563, 572–73 (1935).

58. Ibid., p. 573.

59. Ibid., p. 574.

60. Ibid.

61. Ibid., pp. 574–75.

62. Ibid., pp 575–76.

63. Ibid., pp. 576–77.

64. Ibid., p. 578.

65. Ibid., pp. 578–79.

66. Ibid., p. 579.

67. Record, *Brown v. Mississippi*, p. 179.

68. Meridian *Star*, 29 April 1935, pp. 1, 9.

69. Jackson *Daily News*, 29 April 1935, pp. 1, 8.

70. Jackson *Daily Clarion-Ledger*, 30 April 1935, p. 14.

5

A Question of Money
The NAACP–CIC Connection

Although Earl Brewer had agreed to serve without fee as counsel for Ed Brown, Henry Shields, and Yank Ellington as their case was appealed to the United States Supreme Court, appeals to the Court nonetheless involve expenses other than lawyers' fees, particularly the costs of printing the record of the proceedings in the lower courts, the petition for a writ of certiorari, and the briefs to be filed in the case. A considerable amount of money therefore had to be raised to reimburse Brewer for the expenses the appeal to the Supreme Court would inevitably entail, but despite its pledge to finance the appeal, the National Association for the Advancement of Colored People found itself in financial difficulty when the Mississippi Supreme Court rejected the suggestion of error in the *Brown* case. The result was that the appeal of *Brown* v. *Mississippi* to the Supreme Court was financed with considerable difficulty, and the NAACP became only a part of a coalition that paid for the appeal to the Supreme Court.

The NAACP had, of course, sent John Clark a token payment in the *Brown* case in the summer of 1934. In January 1935, the Clarks advised the association of the status of the case—that a suggestion of error would be filed in the Mississippi Supreme Court by Earl Brewer— and requested that the association pledge a definite sum by which the litigation, including a possible appeal to the U.S. Supreme Court, could be financed. After some negotiations, the NAACP agreed that it would pledge the sum of $500 to finance the *Brown* case, and the association had sent $150 of that pledge to Mississippi prior to the second decision of the Mississippi Supreme Court, rejecting Earl Brewer's suggestion of error. Because of its financially strapped condition, however, the NAACP encountered difficulties in complying further with its $500 pledge, and consequently a financial crisis developed as expenses related to the appeal to the U.S. Supreme Court began to mount during the spring and summer of 1935.[1]

Since the NAACP was apparently unable to finance the appeal to the Supreme Court, it was fortunate for the defense of Brown, Shields, and Ellington that the liberals and moderates in Mississippi had not been alienated from the cause by the manner in which the defense efforts had been conducted, as had been the case in the Scottsboro case. For with the NAACP being almost bankrupt financially as an organization, liberal and moderate forces in Mississippi became crucial to the successful defense of the Kemper County trio, especially in the raising of money.

The Mississippians who played a crucial role in the litigation of *Brown* v. *Mississippi* were associated with the Commission on Interracial Cooperation (CIC), the Atlanta-based interracial organization directed by Will Alexander. The Mississippi CIC had been active in the state, especially in conducting a campaign directed at the prevention of lynching. The Mississippi Bar Association, for example, produced a handbook on the prevention of lynching, which contained contributions from the governor, state judges, and members of Congress, and which was promoted by the Mississippi Interracial Commission as a high-school text.[2]

Will Alexander and the Commission on Interracial Cooperation also encouraged women to join the CIC and support its programs, and for this purpose created a Department of Women's Work. Mrs. Jessie Daniel Ames became the head of the CIC's Department of Women's Work, and in November 1930, she was instrumental in organizing the Association of

Southern Women for the Prevention of Lynching (ASWPL). Since the lynching of blacks was most commonly justified in the South as a means of discouraging the rape of white women, Mrs. Ames concluded that an organization of Southern women would be an effective means of preventing lynching, and in a short time the ASWPL had forty thousand members and had become one of the most effective groups combatting lynching in the South.[3]

Key leaders of the interracial movement in Mississippi were the Right Reverend Theodore D. Bratton, bishop of the Episcopal Diocese of Mississippi, and Mrs. J. Morgan (Ethel Featherstun) Stevens. In addition to his duties as the bishop of the Episcopal Diocese of Mississippi, Rt. Rev. Bratton was a member of the Board of Directors of the Commission on Interracial Cooperation,[4] while Mrs. Stevens was the head of the Association of Southern Women for the Prevention of Lynching in Mississippi. Mrs. Stevens had attended the 1930 Atlanta conference called by Mrs. Ames at which the ASWPL had been founded, and upon her return to Mississippi, she served on the Mississippi State Council of the ASWPL, which by 1935 had succeeded in recruiting members from all but one of the counties in the state.[5]

As it became increasingly clear that the NAACP was experiencing difficulty in raising the necessary money for the appeal of *Brown* v. *Mississippi* to the Supreme Court, alternative sources of support for the litigation had to be found, and the members of the interracial movement in Mississippi provided that support. As his expenses related to the appeal of the *Brown* case to the Supreme Court began to mount, Earl Brewer contacted Bishop Bratton and requested that he use his influence to pressure the NAACP to live up to its financial pledge and to raise other money to meet the expenses of the litigation. Bratton, as it turned out, had already been monitoring the case on behalf of the CIC, and had been especially concerned with the medical condition of Yank Ellington during the period in which he had been denied hospital care in the Hinds County jail in Jackson. A few days after the rejection of the suggestion of error by the Mississippi Supreme Court, Bratton reported to Will Alexander that he was pleased that "Ellington's condition is greatly improved and without complications his life prolonged."[6]

Despite the improvement in Ellington's medical condition, Bratton reported to Alexander, the prospective appeal to the U.S. Supreme Court in the *Brown* case was being seriously jeopardized by lack of money. "In spite of ex-Governor Brewer's most able and truly devoted plea before the Supreme Court of the State," he told Alexander, "the judgment of the lower court has been sustained and the date of execution fixed for June 3rd. Governor Brewer is preparing to appeal the case to the United States [Supreme] Court." This appeal, Bratton pointed out, "will require the expenditure of considerable money and help will be necessary in the raising of it," and in that regard, he indicated, the *Brown* litigation was confronting considerable difficulty.[7]

"I had a long conference with Gov. Brewer this morning [May 3]," Bratton's report to Alexander continued, "and learned these facts: That he came into the case through Mrs. Clark of DeKalb in Kemper County who had had first hand knowledge of the trial, was convinced of the innocence of the Negroes and persuaded him to take the case to the Supreme Court; she also corresponded with the N.A.A.C.P., who promised $500.00 for the prosecution of the case to be sent in installments through Mrs. Clark." Money from the NAACP had been slow in coming, Bratton continued, with the result that Earl Brewer was in the position of bearing considerable expense related to the appeal to the U.S. Supreme Court without being reimbursed. He hoped, Bratton told Alexander, that "your office can help me in awaking the N.A.A.C.P. to the fulfillment of their promise."[8]

"Whatever is done must be done now for the money must be in hand by May the 15th," Bratton concluded. "Gov. Brewer will be at even greater expense, entailing a visit to Washington in addition to the local details incident to the legal procedure. He is perfectly convinced of the innocence of these men and of the cruel injustice of the court procedure thus far. I have asked him to send you a copy of the dissenting opinion of the minority of the [Mississippi Supreme] Court which will be as startling to you as to me."[9]

Although Bishop Bratton had only requested that Will Alexander use his contacts with the NAACP to pressure the association to speed up its financial contributions to the *Brown* appeal, Alexander decided that the case was so important and the financial crisis so serious that he committed the CIC's resources to aid in financing the litigation. Alexander thus telegraphed Bratton on May 6, informing him that the Commission on Interracial Cooperation "will contribute one hundred dollars outright toward [the] expense [of the] appeal mentioned in your letter." In addition, Alexander said, the CIC would "give fifty cents on every dollar coming from other sources provided money from other sources is cleared through our treasury. Simply send check this office. We will immediately send our check for same amount plus fifty per cent."[10] "I hope that in this way," Alexander later wrote Bratton, "we may help to support Governor Brewer in his commendable effort to see that justice is done in what is very clearly a meritorious case."[11]

Alexander also immediately telegraphed Roy Wilkins of the NAACP, advising him that the CIC would add 50 percent to any funds contributed by the NAACP or by any other source for the expenses in the *Brown* case. "This conditional offer," he informed Wilkins, "would apply on any amount you have agreed [to] furnish provided all such funds [are] cleared through our office."[12] Given the serious financial problems confronting the NAACP, Roy Wilkins responded to Alexander's offer of assistance in the *Brown* case with considerable relief. "We are very glad to have this news, because when we assumed financial responsibility for carrying this case to the United States Supreme Court, we really did not have funds in our treasury, but we felt that it was a case we could not afford to turn down," Wilkins wrote Alexander. "We have sent the attorneys a total of $150 to date," Wilkins continued. "It so happened that before your telegram arrived, we had made out a check in the name of John A. Clark, Esq., in the amount of $100, to apply further on the expenses. I am enclosing that check as evidence to your office that such payment is being made, and you can accordingly make an additional contribution of $50. Unless you have a better suggestion as to the handling of the money, we will continue to make our checks out to the attorneys but send them through your office."[13]

Bishop Bratton also responded warmly to Alexander's offer of financial assistance and expressed his gratitude to him "for your generous and prompt response to my letter. I may add that it is also unexpected for my hope was that you would join me in trying to inspirit the N.A.A.C.P. to the fulfillment of their promise." In the meantime, Bratton informed Alexander, he had been active in attempting to raise money for the *Brown* case in Mississippi. He had contacted Mrs. J. Morgan Stevens, the head of the Association of Southern Women for the Prevention of Lynching in Mississippi, Bratton said, and "acquainted her with all the facts known to me. She has agreed to confer with the local women members and endeavor to gain subscribers to the cause."[14]

As Bratton subsequently reported to the CIC and Will Alexander, those primarily responsible for raising funds for the *Brown* case in Mississippi were Mrs. Stevens and Mrs. John Clark, but they were aided by the members of the ASWPL, who raised money in communities around the state, including Jackson, Vicksburg, and Prentiss, while various black organizations also raised some money for the appeal. The efforts, Bratton informed Alexander, were aided by the CIC's "very great help and encouragement, which I verily believe will free these Negroes."[15]

By the spring of 1935, therefore, money to finance the appeal in the *Brown* case began to be contributed from the NAACP, the CIC, and members of the interracial movement in Mississippi sympathetic to the cause of the Kemper trio. In addition, the CIC in Atlanta became the clearinghouse for all funds raised for the appeal, since the commission adhered to Will Alexander's pledge to add 50 percent to any sum forwarded to it from any source, whether the NAACP or contributors in Mississippi. The NAACP contributed the largest amount to the litigation, since the association ultimately forwarded $690 to Earl Brewer through the CIC in Atlanta. Sources in Mississippi, however, almost matched the NAACP's contribution, since a total of $650.21 was raised within the state. The CIC's expenditures involved almost entirely the

TABLE I
Cost of the Proceedings in *Brown* v. *Mississippi*
on Appeal to the U.S. Supreme Court and upon Remand

DATES OF CONTRIBUTIONS	SOURCES OF CONTRIBUTIONS				TOTAL CONTRIBUTIONS
	NAACP	CIC	MISSISSIPPI SOURCES	OTHER	
2 Feb. 1935	$100				$100.00
16 March 1935	50				50.00
10 May 1935	100	$50.00			150.00
18 May 1935		69.25	$138.50		207.75
29 May 1935		45.04	90.08		135.12
19 June 1935		100.00	342.87		442.87
11 July 1935	100	50.00			150.00
16 July 1935	100	50.00			150.00
2 Dec. 1935		10.81	21.62		32.43
20 Dec. 1935		28.57	57.14		85.71
2 Jan. 1936	50	25.00			75.00
7 April 1936	40	20.00			60.00
Spring 1936				11[*]	11.00
16 May 1936	100	100.00			200.00
23 Oct. 1936	50	25.00			75.00
TOTALS	$690	$573.67	$650.21	$11	$1,924.88[†]

[*]On 18 April 1936 Earl Brewer informed the CIC that he had received a check for ten dollars and a one-dollar bill from individuals sympathetic to the Kemper trio in Chapel Hill, N.C., and Cleveland, Ohio.
[†]This total does not include the nominal check the NAACP forwarded to John A. Clark (the sum of which was never specified) in the summer of 1934, nor does it include a sum of $178 that was subsequently forwarded to the Clarks.

matching at the rate of fifty cents on the dollar the sums raised in Mississippi and by the NAACP and the commission's contribution ultimately amounted to $573.67 (see Table 1).[16]

The coalition that supported the litigation in *Brown* v. *Mississippi*, as well as the tactics pursued in that case, were strikingly different from those associated with the Scottsboro case. The campaign of public vilification directed against Alabama by the International Labor Defense had alienated any liberal and moderate forces in Alabama and elsewhere in the South which might otherwise have supported the cause of the Scottsboro defendants, while in the *Brown* case, no such public attacks upon the State of Mississippi or the South had occurred. The *Brown* litigation also did not carry the burden of being directed by a radical, Northern, "outside" group such as the ILD, which openly challenged the system of racial relations in the South and thus alienated any potential Southern support. Although the NAACP formed a part of the coalition supporting the *Brown* case, its presence in the coalition was not publicized in Mississippi, and that fact—in addition to the circumstance that the proceedings against the Kemper trio had been most strongly condemned, not by outside forces, but by two judges of the state supreme court—undoubtedly helped create conditions under which the liberal and moderate Mississippians in the interracial movement could support the *Brown* litigation. And finally, Earl Brewer's leadership of the *Brown* coalition contributed further to the respectability of the cause of the Kemper trio, since he was not only a native Mississippian but also an ex-governor and respected elder statesman, and thus much more acceptable to Mississippians than the Northern lawyers recruited by the ILD to defend the Scottsboro youths were to Alabamians.

There was, nevertheless, a price to be paid for the quiet, nonpublic approach to organizing the defense of the Kemper trio pursued by the NAACP, CIC, and Mississippi interracial leaders, and the price was that in the absence of a publicity campaign, raising money for Brown, Shields, and Ellington was extremely difficult. The total amount of money raised to support the litigation in *Brown* v. *Mississippi* was pitifully small, consisting of slightly less than two thousand dollars. In contrast, the ILD raised over eleven thousand dollars and spent over fourteen thousand dollars on the litigation in *Powell* v. *Alabama* alone.[17]

By mid-May of 1935, the funds being raised by the coalition supporting the *Brown* litigation had begun to reach Mississippi and Will Alexander forwarded to John Clark the $150 that had been jointly furnished by the NAACP and CIC.[18] "We thank you very much for these contributions as these parties are absolutely unable to pay a penny," Clark wrote the CIC, acknowledging his receipt of the money. "We feel like these are very meritorious cases. You know, of course, that it takes a lot of money to carry a case to the United States [Supreme] Court." "On the other hand," Clark continued, "we must remember that three men's lives are involved in this. I am this day endorsing and forwarding the check to Governor Brewer. We feel that these cases will be reversed when they reach the Supreme Court."[19]

The immediate financial crisis that had been hampering the appeal of the *Brown* case was thus overcome. Mrs. J. Morgan Stevens accordingly informed Will Alexander in late May that she had "conferred with Mr. Earl Brewer, counsel for the defense, and he assures me that the case can be handled on the funds we have collected." "The help of the Commission," she added, "has enabled this case to be carried to the U.S. Supreme Court. We of Mississippi are very grateful for that help."[20] "We are very happy to have been able to assist in this case," the CIC responded, "and shall eagerly await a report of the results of the appeal to the United States Supreme Court."[21]

Both Earl Brewer and Mrs. Stevens, as it turned out, were unduly optimistic regarding the cost of the appeal, since in fact the litigation in *Brown* v. *Mississippi* was plagued by subsequent financial emergencies that threatened to seriously hamper the successful prosecution of the case. As early as July 1935, those financing the litigation had difficulty in raising the money to pay for the printing of the record of the proceedings in the Mississippi courts. On July 13, Earl Brewer was constrained to urge the CIC to "hurry [funds] through as quickly as possible, as our time is short." "We are compelled, under the rules of the . . . [Supreme Court] to have this record printed and filed with the Clerk of the United States Supreme Court by the evening of the 28th of this month," Brewer explained, "and it will take several days for it to be printed, so I was compelled to advance to the Clerk of the Court $595 by mailing the Clerk my personal check for the amount." Urging the CIC to speed up the flow of funds to Mississippi, Brewer also expressed his appreciation to the commission "on behalf of Brown, Ellington and Shields, for your cooperation in the matter with Bishop Theodore Bratton, as I do not believe it would have been possible for these boys to have raised the expenses without your assistance."[22]

Brewer also telegraphed the NAACP, urging the association to help pay for the printing of the record and pointing out, incorrectly, that the association had contributed "only a small part" of its $500 pledge. This raised the hackles of Roy Wilkins, who complained to Will Alexander that Brewer was giving the NAACP insufficient credit for its efforts. "Mr. Brewer telegraphs us that we pledged $500 on this case and have contributed 'only a small part,' " Wilkins noted, while in fact the NAACP had contributed a total of $350. "Perhaps he has been misinformed, but it is a little irritating to have this statement sent to us for the second time in the last two months," Wilkins continued. "If you can get over tactfully to him that we are hard pressed and handle many legal cases, and that we are doing what we promised to do, it might help the atmosphere a little."[23]

Despite Wilkins's irritation, the NAACP and the CIC quickly raised funds to help reimburse Brewer for the cost of printing the record, and the record along with a petition for a writ of certiorari was duly filed by Brewer in the Supreme Court on 29 July. The Court should grant the writ of certiorari and reverse the convictions in *Brown* v. *Mississippi,* Brewer argued in his petition, because the convictions of Brown, Shields, and Ellington in the Mississippi courts had been based on coerced confessions and the defendants had been denied the effective assistance of counsel at their trial, all in violation of the Due Process Clause of the Fourteenth Amendment.[24]

Opposing the granting of the writ of certiorari by the Court, the attorney general of Mississippi argued that no federal constitutional questions under the Due Process Clause or otherwise had been raised either in the trial court or in the appeal of the *Brown* case to the Mississippi Supreme Court. The federal constitutional questions under the Due Process Clause, the attorney general argued, had not been raised until the suggestion of error had been filed with the Mississippi Supreme Court. The injection "of a 'federal question' into the case came as an afterthought of counsel," the attorney general said, "and should be treated as such."[25]

The arguments of the Mississippi attorney general proved to be unconvincing, however, since the Supreme Court announced on 14 October that the petition for a writ of certiorari was granted, thus assuring a hearing before the Court on the merits in *Brown* v. *Mississippi.*[26] This was of course welcome news to Earl Brewer and those supporting the appeal, but the granting of certiorari by the Court once again precipitated a financial crisis affecting the litigation, since money now had to be raised to pay for Brewer's trip to Washington to argue the case as well as for printing the brief on the merits.

Once again, Earl Brewer turned to Bishop Bratton for help in raising the money necessary for the continuance of the appeal. Brewer explained to Bratton that the Court had granted certiorari and that the *Brown* case would thus be given a hearing on the merits. "I want to go to Washington and argue this case personally, and ask no pay for any of my time or services, but I will do so simply upon the payment of my traveling expenses and hotel bills and other necessary incidentals," Brewer informed Bratton. "I imagine it would take about $200.00 to cover the balance that is owed to me on the account, to pay for the printing of the brief, and my expenses to Washington and return. I expect . . . [the Court] at a date not far distant to set the case down for hearing, when . . . [the clerk of the Court] will notify me that I must get my brief in at the time required by the . . . [rules] of the Court."[27]

In response to Earl Brewer's appeal for help, Bishop Bratton contacted Roy Wilkins of the NAACP and requested that the association once again raise the necessary funds. "The accounts show that the NAACP has forwarded $300.00 for the prosecution of this case, each of these contributions being supplemented by Dr. Alexander's organization," Bratton wrote Wilkins. "I am therefore referring the completion of this task to your organization. This will be accomplished by the forwarding of the remainder of your $500 subscription which is still due." "May I add that our local organization has pretty fully exhausted its efforts, having appealed successfully to our clientele and having raised and delivered rather more than our expectancy," Bratton pointed out. "I think no time ought to be lost in bringing this case to its conclusion. Governor Brewer has been wise, diligent and successful so far and his concluding efforts should suffer no handicap."[28]

Wilkins was again irritated by Bratton's letter, since the NAACP had in fact contributed $450 of the $500 it had pledged for the *Brown* litigation and thus did not still owe $200 as

Bratton had indicated. Consequently Wilkins responded to Bratton's appeal on November 14, detailing the NAACP's role in the litigation and pointing out that the association owed only $50 on its $500 pledge. "It is true that in our letter of January 31, [1935] while we made it clear that we were not pledging more than $500, we did say that we would attempt to raise additional funds if they became necessary," Wilkins wrote Bratton. "We must have anticipated our present straightened circumstances with clairvoyancy, because at the present time we would be hard pressed, indeed, to raise $100 more on this case." "The most that I can promise for the moment," Wilkins continued, "is that we will send our balance due of $50 through the Interracial Commission, if they will continue their arrangement of paying 50¢ for every dollar sent them."[29]

That would result in the immediate forwarding to Earl Brewer of $75, Wilkins pointed out, but he admitted that he was at a loss as to how the remainder of the cost of the appeal was to be met. "For the balance of $125 which . . . [Earl Brewer] estimates is needed in order for him to go to Washington and argue the case, and bear other incidental expenses," Wilkins said, "I can say only that we will try to raise some of this money, but I must be frank and state that the outlook is not promising. Whatever we do raise, of course, we will send through the Interracial Commission so that they can supplement it."[30]

Wilkins concluded by expressing his appreciation to Bratton "for the very material aid your forces have given in this important case," and he expressed his regret that "at the time when we are almost to press for a decision our funds are so greatly depleted." The NAACP, he added, "suspended several months ago any further commitments in legal cases, because we did not have the money and did not see where we could get it."[31]

At what was perhaps the most crucial stage in the litigation of *Brown* v. *Mississippi*, therefore, the appeal to the Supreme Court appeared to be in real jeopardy because of the lack of a relatively small amount of money. Bishop Bratton communicated to Earl Brewer the gloomy news that the NAACP could contribute only $50, and expressed the hope that the CIC would supplement that sum with an additional $25. "This means that we will have to find from some source [the] $125.00 needed to complete the appeal to the Supreme Court," Bratton wrote Brewer. "Frankly I do not know just where we are to get it, but I am at once making the effort."[32]

Bishop Bratton related the details of the latest financial emergency facing the *Brown* case in a letter to Will Alexander on 22 November, pointing out that Roy Wilkins "seems to think that your offer holds good to add 50¢ on every dollar raised." "If this is true it will be a great help," he added. "Mrs. [J. Morgan] Stevens and I in our former effort had about exhausted our list of possibilities. I have asked Mr. Wilkins to make the strongest plea he can and endeavor to raise the $125.00 needed to complete the case and when this is done report to me and I will make every effort to raise the balance."[33] The CIC replied to Bratton in early December, assuring him that the commission's offer to add 50 percent to any amount raised for the *Brown* case still stood. "We hope," the CIC said, "that it will be possible to secure the full amount needed."[34]

The NAACP was nonetheless able to contribute only the $50 that remained of its $500 pledge. In late December, Earl Brewer informed the association by telegram that the Supreme Court had granted certiorari and that the oral argument in the *Brown* case had been set for 9 January 1936. "Must have money for printing of brief and trip to Washington for argument immediately if case is to be successfully concluded," Brewer informed the NAACP. "How about $150 balance on your $500 promise?" The association replied, however, that it was "sending check today Interracial Commission for $50 balance we owe you asking Commission [to] add their contribution and forward check to you for $75. This is utmost we can pay today." And the NAACP complained to the CIC that "Mr. Brewer seems to have difficulty in getting clearly in mind how much is due him."[35] The result was that Earl Brewer received only $75 from outside Mississippi to help defray the cost of the final stage of the appeal.[36]

Bishop Bratton and Mrs. Stevens discovered, on the other hand, that money could be raised within the state only with extreme difficulty. "It has been somewhat difficult to get the interest of people just at this time, when, on every street corner, appeals are being made by the Salvation Army, the Welfare Association, Committees on Local Relief, the Red Cross and other agencies," Bratton reported to Will Alexander. Bratton and Mrs. Stevens therefore personally contributed a total of $57.14 to the cause, and with the CIC matching this amount at fifty cents on the dollar, $85.71 was paid to Earl Brewer.[37]

At this juncture, Mississippi blacks were also able to contribute to the case. Earl Brewer reported to Bishop Bratton that "some colored men came in and left in my office for me, in the Ed Brown, Henry Shields, and Yank Ellington case, $21.62." "This was left in small amounts," Brewer said, "$11.01 from one party, $6.81 from another party, $1.80 from another and $2.00 from another." These unexpected contributions were immediately sent to the CIC, which added 50 percent to the sum and forwarded $32.43 to Brewer. In this rather painful manner, the amount that Earl Brewer estimated he needed to complete the appeal was almost, although not completely, met.[38]

As *Brown* v. *Mississippi* was pending before the Supreme Court, the press in Mississippi began to express uneasiness over the effect the Kemper County trio's case might have upon the state's national image, as the case was increasingly referred to as the "Mississippi Scottsboro Case." The Jackson *Daily Clarion-Ledger* reported that the case of the Kemper trio was a "story that interested most Mississippians" during the spring of 1935. "The fear and prospect," the *Clarion-Ledger* added, "that it may develop into another 'Scottsboro Case' increased this interest."[39]

This uneasiness of the Mississippi press reflected the fact that the Scottsboro case in Alabama had become a national cause célèbre under the direction of the International Labor Defense. Alabama's insistence on retrying and reconvicting the Scottsboro defendants, after the U. S. Supreme Court had reversed the original convictions in *Powell* v. *Alabama* in 1932, only served to increase the widespread condemnations of Alabama justice. Indeed, the Communist Party and the International Labor Defense were able to make the Scottsboro case the subject of worldwide protests against racial injustice in the South, and the press in Mississippi obviously feared that Mississippi might also become the object of similar attacks and condemnations as a result of *Brown* v. *Mississippi*.[40]

To the undoubted relief of the Mississippi press and officialdom, however, the Kemper County trio's case never attracted the spotlight of national attention that had focused upon the Alabama Scottsboro case. There were no demonstrations at the White House or the Congress, parades in New York City, or protests in Europe regarding the proceedings against Brown, Shields, and Ellington, in contrast to the response to the Scottsboro litigation. The low-profile approach to organizing the defense of the Kemper trio by the coalition supporting their cause resulted in a virtually total publicity blackout. With the exception of items regarding the *Brown* case in its monthly publication, the *Crisis*, the NAACP did not extensively publicize the litigation, and the CIC similarly did not attempt to either generate support or raise money for the cause by publicizing its role in the litigation. The case of the Kemper County trio, as a consequence, remained largely invisible in terms of national publicity as it proceeded to the Supreme Court.

An exception to this generalization occurred, however, when the *Brown* case attracted the attention of the *Nation*, a leading liberal publication. The *Nation* published an article regarding the case in December 1935, based largely on the dissenting opinion of Judge Virgil Griffith of the Mississippi Supreme Court. The article detailed the brutal torture to which Brown, Shields, and Ellington had been subjected by Deputy Sheriff Cliff Dial and others in forcing them to confess, and denounced the proceedings in the case in scathing terms. "The technique of crime detection among the Negro population in Kemper and Lauderdale counties, Mississippi, was disclosed during the cross-examination [at the trial]," the *Nation* said. "The confession is obtained by the deputy or deputies in the fashion indicated above. Then the sheriff is called in to hear it. He goes through the perfunctory gestures of his office, tells the accused to disclose the truth, says the law is there to protect the accused and so on." "His hands are thus kept clean," the *Nation* pointed out. "The dirty work is done by deputies and the blood mopped up before the sheriff arrives. Bruises, lacerations, even necks burned by the noose are overlooked, or credited perhaps to misadventure before the accused was taken under the protection of the law." Greater injustice in the case had been avoided, the *Nation* indicated, by John Clark's courage in appealing the convictions of the Kemper trio, and Judge Griffith was also praised for his eloquent dissenting opinion in the state supreme court.[41]

The *Nation* subsequently named John A. Clark and Judge Virgil Griffith to the magazine's "Honor Roll,"[42] and the publication of the article on the Kemper trio's case additionally produced some much-needed moral support, as well as financial contributions, to John Clark and his wife. J. M. Kaplan, of New York City, for example, read the article in the *Nation* and wrote to Mrs. Clark that it seemed to him "that the aims and accomplishments of your husband are equal to the attainments of the best that has been realized and credited to any individual on this earth. Therefore, I pray for the continuation of his strength in order that he may courageously carry on his good work." "At the same time," Kaplan added, "I want to commend you for the great part in his life and for humanity at large which you yourself are contributing, in a similar and difficult path." Kaplan enclosed a fifty-dollar contribution to the defense of the Kemper County trio,[43] and he also contacted Arthur Garfield Hays, the well-known New York civil-liberties lawyer, and informed him of the case. "I do not know how much money will be required to pay for the services of the criminal lawyer in the State of Mississippi who is to be engaged to carry on the fight for the poor, outraged three Negroes," Kaplan wrote Hays, "and it seems to me that you would be the best individual to procure subscriptions for that purpose."[44]

As it turned out, Hays had also read the *Nation* article and had already written the Clarks, enclosing his own contribution to the defense of Brown, Shields, and Ellington. "I was so moved by the story," Hays said, "and by . . . [John Clark's] nobility and self-sacrifice, that I wrote him a letter and enclosed a small check toward the defense fund."[45] "Your letter with check," Mrs. Clark wrote Hays, "coming just as Mr. Clark is recovering from a long and critical illness, is deeply appreciated." "I am sure that your letter is going to do lots toward helping to brighten my husband's convalescing days," she added. "I would appreciate you having other friends write Mr. Clark; the letters will strengthen his determination to get well and renew the fight with courage and the consciousness that he is upholding the high standard of the legal profession."[46]

Hays acted upon J. M. Kaplan's suggestion and solicited other individuals for contributions to the defense of the Kemper trio, with the result that several additional checks were received by the Clarks. "I wish I could adequately express how deeply Mr. Clark and I appreciate your interest in 'the negro case,' which has caused us so much worry and unhappiness," Mrs. Clark wrote Hays. "Since the article appeared in the 'Nation' we have received many letters and a few telegrams from readers who wanted to express their commendation for the fight Mr. Clark has made." "A majority of the letters, tho'," she continued, "were written by friends you had contacted and whose interest you have enlisted. Some of the writers have sent checks to the total of $178.00. This money, which is indeed a God send, I am placing in a separate account to be used solely for the defense of the negroes."[47]

"I have reached the conclusion that all of my public welfare and political activities are to be the means for giving me prestige and contacts I shall need for what I have decided to do in the future," Mrs. Clark told Hays. "I shall from now on be active in helping the poor unfortunate negroes in their vain efforts to secure justice in Courts. This case has brought to me the realization that we are our brother's keeper and I feel that it is my duty to help the unfortunate victims of race hatred and prejudice." "We have paid a great price for being true to our conception of duty," she concluded, "and I know that the future will bring more disappointments and unhappiness because of our stand in face of so much local prejudice and intolerance, but you can be assured that we will always be fighting for the cause in which you have manifested a friendly interest."[48]

Part of the great price that the Clarks had paid as a result of their involvement in the defense of Brown, Shields, and Ellington was the destruction of what had once appeared to be a promising political career for John Clark. For, in the summer of 1935, as Earl Brewer prepared to appeal the *Brown* case to the U.S. Supreme Court, John Clark was defeated for reelection to the Mississippi senate in the Democratic primaries. "The only issue in the campaign," Mrs. Clark said, "was his defense of the negroes."[49]

At least for the Clarks, the personal cost of the litigation in *Brown* v. *Mississippi* undoubtedly overshadowed the difficulties that had beset the marshaling of the monetary resources necessary to finance the appeal. John Clark was now out of the fight over the fate of the Kemper County trio, but Earl Brewer had persuaded the Supreme Court to grant certiorari in *Brown* v. *Mississippi,* and the scene of the battle shifted from Mississippi to Washington, D.C.

1. Roy Wilkins to Theodore D. Bratton, 14 Nov. 1935, CIC Papers.

2. George Brown Tindall, *The Emergence of the New South* (Baton Rouge: Louisiana State University Press, 1967), p. 179.

3. See Jacquelyn Dowd Hall, *Revolt against Chivalry: Jessie Daniel Ames and the Women's Campaign against Lynching* (New York: Columbia University Press, 1979).

4. Wilma Dykeman and James Stokely, *Seeds of Southern Change: The Life of Will Alexander* (Chicago: University of Chicago Press, 1962), p. 157.

5. Hall, *Revolt against Chivalry,* p. 173.

6. Theodore D. Bratton to Will Alexander, 3 May 1935, CIC Papers.

7. Ibid.

8. Ibid.

9. Ibid.

10. Will Alexander to Theodore D. Bratton, 6 May 1935, CIC Papers.

11. Will Alexander to Theodore D. Bratton, 7 May 1935, ibid.

12. Will Alexander to Roy Wilkins, 6 May 1935, ibid.

13. Roy Wilkins to Will Alexander, 7 May 1935, ibid.

14. Theodore D. Bratton to Will Alexander 7 May 1935, ibid.

15. Theodore D. Bratton to Will Alexander, 19 June 1935, ibid.

16. These figures are based on the sums mentioned in the correspondence in the CIC Papers.

17. Memorandum of ILD Receipts and Expenditures, ACLU Archives, vol. 646. 31 Dec. 1932.

18. Will Alexander to John A. Clark, 13 May 1935, CIC Papers.

19. John A. Clark to CIC, 15 May 1935, ibid.

20. Mrs. J. Morgan Stevens to Will Alexander, 20 May 1935, ibid.

21. Emily H. Clay to Mrs. J. Morgan Stevens, 29 May 1935, ibid.

22. Earl Brewer to CIC, 13 July 1935, ibid.

23. Roy Wilkins to Will Alexander, 11 July 1935, ibid.

24. Petition for a Writ of Certiorari, Record, *Brown* v. *Mississippi*, p. 2.

25. Brief in Opposition to Granting Certiorari, Record, *Brown* v. *Mississippi*, p. 4.

26. 296 U.S. 560 (1935).

27. Quoted in Theodore D. Bratton to Roy Wilkins, 12 Nov. 1935, CIC Papers.

28. Ibid.

29. Roy Wilkins to Theodore D. Bratton, 14 Nov. 1935, ibid.

30. Ibid.

31. Ibid.

32. Theodore D. Bratton to Earl Brewer, 22 Nov. 1935, ibid.

33. Theodore D. Bratton to Will Alexander, 22 Nov. 1935, ibid.

34. Emily H. Clay to Theodore D. Bratton, 2 Dec. 1935, ibid.

35. Walter White to CIC, 30 Dec. 1935, ibid.

36. Emily H. Clay to Earl Brewer, 2 Jan. 1936, ibid.

37. Theodore D. Bratton to Will Alexander, 16 Dec. 1935; Emily H. Clay to Theodore D. Bratton, 20 Dec. 1935, ibid.

38. Earl Brewer to Theodore D. Bratton, 18 Dec. 1935; Emily H. Clay to Earl Brewer, 20 Dec. 1935; Earl Brewer to Will Alexander, 26 Dec. 1935, ibid.

39. Jackson *Daily Clarion-Ledger*, 5 May 1935, p. 6.

40. See Dan T. Carter, *Scottsboro: A Tragedy of the American South*, rev. ed. (Baton Rouge: Louisiana State University Press); Jackson *Daily Clarion-Ledger*, 12 Jan. 1936, p. 6, editorial, "A New Trial for These Three Would Be Welcome in Mississippi"; see also "Another Scottsboro Case," *New Republic* 85 (13 Nov. 1935): 19.

41. Robert W. Horton, "Not Too Much for a Negro," *Nation* 141 (11 Dec. 1935): 674–76.

42. *Nation* 142 (1, Jan. 1936): 9.

43. J. M. Kaplan to Mrs. John A. Clark, 6 Jan. 1936, ACLU Archives, Vol. 941.

44. J. M. Kaplan to Arthur Garfield Hays, 6 Jan. 1936, ibid.

45. Arthur Garfield Hays to Roger Baldwin, 10 Jan. 1936, ibid.

46. Mrs. John A. Clark to Arthur Garfield Hays, 12 Dec. 1935, ibid.

47. Mrs. John A. Clark to Arthur Garfield Hays, 21 Jan. 1936, ibid.

48. Ibid.

49. Ibid.; Meridian *Star*, 8 Aug. 1935, p. 7; 28 Aug. 1935, p. 1.

6

The Quiet of a Storm Center

The *Brown* Case and the New Deal Court

When Earl Brewer's petition for a writ of certiorari in *Brown* v. *Mississippi* arrived at the United States Supreme Court at the end of July 1935, the Court was on the eve of a major change in its institutional setting. For seventy-five years, the Court had sat in the old Senate chamber in the Capitol, but Chief Justice William Howard Taft had believed that the Court, as one of the three coordinate branches of the national government, deserved its own building. By engaging in an intensive lobbying campaign, Taft was able to secure congressional authorization for the acquisition of a site for a Supreme Court building in 1925, and finally in 1929 Congress appropriated almost ten million dollars for construction. "My prayer is," Taft said, "that I may stay long enough on the Court to see that building constructed. If I do, then I shall have the right to claim that it was my work, for without me it certainly would not have been taken up at this time." His death in 1930 ended Taft's hope to see the Court in its new quarters, but the building, located across the street from the Capitol, was finally completed in 1935, and the Court opened its term in October 1935 quartered in what some critics called its "marble palace."[1]

Although Taft's dream had finally become a reality, some

of the justices were uncomfortable in the new building and continued to work at home as they had in the past. And Associate Justice Harlan Fiske Stone was rather critical of the Court's new home. "It is a very grand affair, but I confess that I returned from my visit with a feeling akin to dismay," Stone wrote privately. "The place is almost bombastically pretentious, and thus seems to me wholly inappropriate for a quiet group of old boys such as the Supreme Court of the United States. In my brief inspection I discovered many inconveniences, due to bad plans and lack of criticism of the plans by the people who are to use the building. It seems a great pity that the United States should spend $10,000,000 upon a building, constructed to last forever, but exhibiting such grave faults."[2]

The Supreme Court may have consisted of a "quiet group of old boys," but, as Justice Oliver Wendell Holmes had said, although it might be quiet at the Court, it was the "quiet of a storm centre."[3] By the fall of 1935, adjusting to their new quarters was the least of the problems concerning the members of the Supreme Court, since the Court was by then well down the path toward being the center of a new storm of controversy involving a constitutional confrontation with President Roosevelt and the New Deal.

The Court that moved into the new building in the fall of 1935 was significantly different from the solidly conservative Court over which Chief Justice Taft had presided during the 1920s. In addition to living to see the new Court building completed, Taft had hoped that he and his conservative colleagues would live to control the Court's decisions in the 1930s as they had in the 1920s. Writing in 1929, Taft had expressed the hope for "continued life of enough of the present membership . . . to prevent disastrous reversals of our present attitude." With Justices Willis Van Devanter, James McReynolds, George Sutherland, Pierce Butler, and Edward Sanford forming a staunch conservative bloc on the Court, Taft observed, "there will be five to steady the boat. . .we must not all give up at once." But like his hope to live to see the new Supreme Court building completed, Taft's desire to see the Court continue to be dominated by a solid conservative majority was not to be, since both he and Justice Sanford died in 1930.[4]

The Court that considered the arguments in *Brown* v. *Mississippi* in 1936 was therefore a significantly different Court from the Taft Court of the 1920s, as President Hoover had replaced Taft as Chief Justice with Charles Evans Hughes and Justice Sanford with Owen J. Roberts. The appointments of Hughes and Roberts shifted the center of gravity on the Court and reduced the solid conservative wing of the Court to four justices. The result was a more moderate Court, with Chief Justice Hughes and Justice Roberts as the "swing men" whose votes could tip the decisions of the Court either to the conservative or liberal side.[5]

Justices Sutherland, Van Devanter, McReynolds, and Butler nevertheless continued to form a cohesive conservative bloc on the Court during the 1930s, and unfortunately for many of the most important pieces of Roosevelt's New Deal legislation, Chief Justice Hughes and Justice Roberts from 1933 to 1936 voted with the "Four Horsemen"—as the conservatives were called—to declare unconstitutional many of the most important programs of the New Deal. The Court's decisions invalidating New Deal programs were frequently protested by the liberal bloc on the Court—Justices Louis D. Brandeis, Harlan Fiske Stone, and Benjamin N. Cardozo—and these protests were echoed both in the administration and the Congress, as the debate over the proper role of the Court became increasingly acrimonious not only in the government but in the country at large.[6]

The Court was composed of "nine old men" throwing up roadblocks to progressive reforms, the critics charged, while the Court's defenders portrayed the justices as neutral and virtuous guardians of eternal constitutional verities. By 1936, there were forty legislative proposals pending in Congress directed at removing the Court as a roadblock to the New Deal, and patience with the Court was obviously wearing thin in liberal circles.[7] Reacting to the Court's decision invalidating the New Deal's basic farm program in 1936, the *Nation* declared that it "is inconceivable that the good sense of a democracy will tolerate very much longer such use of judicial power." "If Mr. Roosevelt has courage he will make the limitation of this power in declaring acts unconstitutional a major part of his [1936 reelection] campaign," the *Nation* continued. "If he has a long view of statesmanship he will make it part of a long-range effort to restore basic decisions of a democracy to the legislative will of the people."[8]

The scope and legitimacy of governmental power to regulate property rights and to direct the national economy formed the central constitutional issue in the debate over the validity of the New Deal. Largely obscured by the controversy surrounding the New Deal was the fact that the Court had only recently initiated a constitutional development of lasting significance for the future by strengthening the protection of civil liberties under the Constitution. This development had its roots in decisions of the Taft Court, but it was accelerated and expanded by the Court under the leadership of Chief Justice Hughes.

This expansion of the constitutional protection of civil liberties involved the interpretation of the Due Process Clause of the Fourteenth Amendment to impose upon the states restrictions either similar or identical to those rights secured in the Bill of Rights. The Court had held in *Barron* v. *Baltimore* in 1833 that the guarantees of personal liberty in the Bill of Rights were restrictions on the power of the national government alone and were inapplicable to the states.[9] But after the adoption of the Fourteenth Amendment as a restriction on state power in 1868, the Court had been urged time and again to accept the view that the Due Process Clause of the Fourteenth Amendment applied to the states some or all of the guarantees of the Bill of Rights. In contrast to its willingness to use the Due Process Clause to protect substantive economic and property rights, however, the Court proved to be extremely reluctant to interpret the Fourteenth Amendment as guaranteeing against state action either the substantive rights, such as freedom of speech, or the criminal-procedure protections contained in the Bill of Rights. Indeed, in *Hurtado* v. *California*, decided in 1884, the Court rejected the argument that the Due Process Clause required the states to initiate

proceedings in serious criminal cases by grand jury indictments, as the Fifth Amendment of the Bill of Rights required
of the federal government, and the Court additionally adopted
reasoning in the *Hurtado* case that denied that the Due Process
Clause could guarantee against the states rights either similar
or identical to those in the Bill of Rights.[10]

In *Twining* v. *New Jersey* in 1908, the Court also rejected
an argument that the Due Process Clause of the Fourteenth
Amendment imposed upon the states the right against compulsory self-incrimination, a right also guaranteed by the Fifth
Amendment of the Bill of Rights and thus applicable in federal
criminal proceedings. The concept of due process of law and
the right against compulsory self-incrimination, the Court
held in the *Twining* case, had emerged independently of each
other in English law, with the result that the right against
compulsory self-incrimination could not be said to be an in-
herent element of the concept of due process. The right against
compulsory self-incrimination, the Court said, had come "into
existence not as an essential part of due process, but as a wise
and beneficent rule of evidence developed in the courts in the
course of judicial decision." "The right against self-incrimination is not fundamental to due process of law, nor an essential
part of it," the Court concluded, and the "exemption from
compulsory self-incrimination in the courts of the states is not
secured by any part of the Federal Constitution."[11]

Although under the Court's decision in the *Twining* case,
there was no right against self-incrimination in state proceedings under the Due Process Clause of the Fourteenth Amendment, the Court did open the door in the *Twining* case to the
possibility that the Due Process Clause might in the future be
interpreted to guarantee at least some rights similar to those in
the Bill of Rights. It was possible, the Court said in the
Twining case, "that some of the personal rights safeguarded by
the first eight Amendments [the Bill of Rights] against national
action may also be safeguarded against state action, because a
denial of them would be a denial of due process of law."
Whether a right similar to one in the Bill of Rights applied to
the states via the Due Process Clause, the Court said, depended upon this question: "Is it a fundamental principle of

liberty and justice which inheres in the very idea of free government and is the inalienable right of a citizen of such a government?"[12]

While the Court held in the *Twining* case that the right against compulsory self-incrimination was not such a fundamental principle of liberty and justice, its general discussion of the meaning of the Due Process Clause left open the possibility that rights at least similar to some of the other rights in the Bill of Rights might be held to be guarantees against state action in the future. The Court therefore seemed to have moved away from the holding in the *Hurtado* case, in which it had denied that the Due Process Clause could guarantee rights either similar or identical to those in the Bill of Rights.

After the Court had indicated that the Due Process Clause had a potential for growth in the direction of protecting civil liberties, there were nevertheless no decisions by the Court fulfilling the promise of the *Twining* case until the 1920s. Then, in its 1925 decision in *Gitlow* v. *New York*, the Court declared that for "present purposes we may and do assume that freedom of speech and of the press—which are protected by the 1st Amendment from abridgment by Congress—are among the fundamental personal rights and 'liberties' protected by the due process clause of the 14th Amendment from impairment by the states."[13] Although it was unclear after the *Gitlow* case whether the Court had only assumed that freedom of speech and of the press were protected by the Due Process Clause for the purpose of deciding that case, the decision in fact marked a major departure in the interpretation of the Due Process Clause and what would later be called the nationalization of the Bill of Rights as restrictions upon state power. For in *Stromberg* v. *California*[14] and *Near* v. *Minnesota*,[15] both decided in 1931, Chief Justice Hughes explicitly acknowledged what the Court had only assumed in the *Gitlow* case—that freedom of speech and freedom of the press were henceforth to be considered guarantees of the Due Process Clause as restrictions upon the powers of the states. Writing for a unanimous Court in 1936, Justice Sutherland could therefore accurately declare that freedom of speech and freedom of the press had been held to be guarantees of the Due Process Clause in a "a series of decisions of this court, beginning with *Gitlow* v. *New York* . . . and ending with *Near* v. *Minnesota* . . . ." [16]

This expansion of the Due Process Clause of the Fourteenth Amendment to protect the substantive rights of free speech and freedom of the press was paralleled by an almost simultaneous expansion of the Due Process Clause to impose procedural restrictions upon state criminal proceedings. Just as the Court had refused to hold that the Due Process Clause guaranteed rights similar to those in the First Amendment until the *Gitlow* case in 1925, it had also initially denied that the Due Process Clause imposed upon state criminal trials procedural restrictions similar to those found in the Bill of Rights. The Court had thus refused to compel the states to initiate criminal proceedings by grand jury indictments in the *Hurtado* case in 1884, and in subsequent cases it had held that the states need not under the Due Process Clause employ twelve-person juries in criminal cases,[17] although the Sixth Amendment required such juries in federal criminal trials; that the Cruel and Unusual Punishment Clause of the Eighth Amendment,[18] and the right of confrontation and cross-examination guaranteed by the Sixth Amendment, did not apply to the states;[19] and, in *Twining* v. *New Jersey,* that the Self-Incrimination Clause of the Fifth Amendment was also inapplicable in a state proceeding. In the *Twining* case, as well as in the earlier case of *Spies* v. *Illinois,*[20] the Court additionally rejected arguments that the Due Process Clause of the Fourteenth Amendment applied all of the Bill of Rights to the states.

As late as 1915 in *Frank* v. *Mangum,* the Court indicated that the Due Process Clause required of the states only that they provide criminal defendants with adequate notice of the charges against them and an opportunity to be heard according to the traditional modes of proceeding in such cases. Even if allegations of grave violations of procedural fairness were made regarding a state criminal trial, the Court held, the Due Process Clause was satisfied if the states afforded a "corrective process," such as appellate review in the state courts, through which such allegations could be reviewed. And the decisions of the state courts regarding violations of due process in state criminal proceedings, the Court indicated, were to be treated as virtually conclusive as far as the federal courts were concerned.[21]

In 1923, however, the Supreme Court decided *Moore* v. *Dempsey*,[22] a case that proved to be a turning point in the Court's interpretation of the Due Process Clause in relation to state criminal proceedings. For in the *Moore* case, the Court proved to be willing to look beyond the mere forms of proceedings in state criminal trials and to inquire whether state criminal defendants had in fact been afforded fair trials in the state courts. And if a denial of fundamental fairness had occurred—such as mob domination of a trial, the issue in the *Moore* case—the Court indicated that the resolution of allegations of unfairness by the state courts would not henceforth be treated as virtually conclusive as had been the case in *Frank* v. *Mangum*. If a criminal defendant were denied a fair trial in the state courts in violation of the Due Process Clause, the Court said in the *Moore* case, even "perfection in the machinery for correction" supplied in the state courts would not "prevent . . . [the Supreme Court] from securing to the petitioners their constitutional rights."[23]

What had thus begun to emerge in the decision in *Moore* v. *Dempsey* came to be called the fair-trial rule under the Due Process Clause—a rule that required the states to afford criminal defendants fair trials in fact, not just in form. Although it was clear from the *Moore* case that a trial dominated by a mob was not a fair trial as required by the Due Process Clause, the next problem confronting the Court was the determination of what other procedural elements constituted a fair trial. And in making that determination, the Court expanded the meaning of the Due Process Clause and incrementally increased the restrictions that the federal Constitution imposed on the conduct of state criminal trials.

In *Tumey* v. *Ohio*, decided in 1927, the Court held that the Due Process Clause required that unbiased judges must preside in state proceedings, and that a judge who had a pecuniary interest in convicting defendants could not conduct a fair trial as required by the Due Process Clause.[24] More importantly, however, the Court ruled in 1932 in the first Scottsboro case,

Powell v. *Alabama,* that the effective assistance of counsel, at least in a capital case, was essential to the due process guarantee of a fair trial in a state court. If indigent defendants were involved in a capital case in a state court, the Court held, the failure of the state to appoint counsel to represent them would violate the Due Process Clause.[25]

By 1935, the Court was pointing out that the traditional view, that due process in a criminal trial merely entailed the right to notice of the charges and an opportunity to be heard, was no longer acceptable. Rejecting an argument presenting the traditional view in *Mooney* v. *Holohan,* the Court stated that it was "unable to approve this narrow view of the requirement of due process." "That requirement, in safeguarding the liberty of the citizen against deprivation through the action of the State," the Court continued, "embodies the fundamental conceptions of justice which lie at the base of our civil and political institutions." The Court further held that the knowing use of perjured testimony to convict a criminal defendant in a state court, as charged in the *Mooney* case, constituted a denial of due process of law. Due process, the court declared, "is a requirement that cannot be deemed to be satisfied by mere notice and hearing if a State has contrived a conviction through the pretence of a trial which in truth is but used as a means of depriving a defendant of liberty through a deliberate deception of court and jury by the presentation of testimony known to be perjured." "Such a contrivance by a State to procure the conviction and imprisonment of a defendant," the Court concluded, "is as inconsistent with the rudimentary demands of justice as is the obtaining of a like result by intimidation."[26]

When *Brown* v. *Mississippi* was appealed to the Supreme Court in the fall of 1935, the path of due process under the Fourteenth Amendment had therefore only relatively recently turned in a new direction. The Court had not only begun the nationalization of rights in the First Amendment, making them applicable to the states via the Due Process Clause, but it had also begun to refine the meaning of the fair-trial rule that had emerged in *Moore* v. *Dempsey,* with the result that new restrictions were being imposed upon state criminal proceedings. By the time of the *Brown* appeal, the Due Process Clause pro-

hibited the states from convicting defendants in mob-dominated trials and from using perjured testimony to secure convictions, and it additionally required the states to appoint
counsel for indigent defendants in capital cases, while also
furnishing an unbiased judge in criminal trials.

In imposing these new restrictions upon state criminal
trials, however, the Court was not applying the procedural
rights in the Bill of Rights to the states. The right to counsel
that the Court had found to be required by the Due Process
Clause in *Powell* v. *Alabama* was only similar but not identical
to the right to counsel in the Sixth Amendment of the Bill of
Rights and applicable in federal criminal proceedings.[27] The
states were required to appoint counsel for indigent defendants
in capital cases, the Court had held, not because the Sixth
Amendment's provision for the right to counsel was applicable
to the states but rather because representation by counsel in a
capital case was essential to a fair trial as required by the Due
Process Clause. In tightening the due-process restrictions applicable in state criminal cases, the Court was therefore following the reasoning in the *Twining* case—that the Due Process
Clause imposed upon state proceedings some rights similar but
not identical to those in the Bill of Rights. And in addition, the
Court was holding that under the fair-trial rule certain practices, such as mob domination of a trial or the knowing use of
perjured testimony, which were nowhere condemned in the
Bill of Rights in specific terms, were nevertheless incompatible
with the right to a fair trial under the Due Process Clause.[28]

This new departure under the Due Process Clause of the
Fourteenth Amendment involving the imposition of restrictions on state criminal procedure was of course crucial to the
outcome in *Brown* v. *Mississippi*, but also of great significance
were the voting patterns on the Court in state criminal cases
arising under the Due Process Clause. Although the conservative bloc on the Court, for example, opposed most New
Deal measures with virtual unanimity, the same cohesiveness
among the views of the conservatives did not exist in the state
criminal-procedure cases. All four members of the conservative
bloc had in fact been on the Court when the breakthrough case
of *Moore* v. *Dempsey* was decided in 1923, but only Justices

McReynolds and Sutherland had dissented from Justice Holmes's opinion for the Court, while Justices Butler and Van Devanter voted with the majority.[29] The court's decisions in *Tumey* v. *Ohio* and in *Mooney* v. *Holohan,* on the other hand, were unanimous, with all of the Four Horsemen supporting the result. And in *Powell* v. *Alabama,* only Justices Butler and McReynolds dissented, while Justice Sutherland wrote the majority opinion, supported not only by Chief Justice Hughes and Justices Roberts, Brandeis, Stone, and Cardozo but also by Justice Van Devanter, who had been Chief Justice Taft's right-hand man on the Court during the 1920s.[30]

The rather predictable bloc voting on the Supreme Court that frequently occurred when cases involving economic issues arose during the 1930s did not prevail in cases concerning criminal procedure under the Due Process Clause. In economic cases, the Four Horsemen could almost always be found united in opposition to governmental regulation of economic rights, the liberals—Brandeis, Stone and Cardozo—generally supportive of governmental regulation, and Chief Justice Hughes and Justice Roberts holding the balance of power between the two blocs. As is sometimes the case when the Court confronts novel issues, however, voting patterns in criminal-procedure cases during the 1930s were much less predictable than in cases presenting more settled issues.[31]

Perhaps no case epitomized this point more than the Court's 1934 decision in *Snyder* v. *Massachusetts.*[32] At issue was whether a defendant was entitled to accompany a jury when the jury viewed the scene of the alleged crime during the conduct of a state criminal trial. Although all members of the Court agreed that the issue was whether the right to a fair trial was denied under the Due Process Clause if a defendant were denied the right to accompany the jury on a view, the Court nevertheless divided five to four on the issue in the *Synder* case. And the voting behavior of the justices deviated almost completely from the bloc voting patterns in economic cases.

Justice Cardozo, a member of the liberal bloc, wrote the majority opinion, rejecting the claim that the Due Process Clause had been violated in the *Snyder* case. Joining Cardozo were Chief Justice Hughes and Justices Stone, Van Devanter, and McReynolds. The dissenting opinion was written by Justice Roberts, who normally voted with Chief Justice Hughes; Roberts's dissent was joined by the leader of the liberal bloc, Justice Brandeis, and by the conservative justices Sutherland and Butler.[33]

Both the doctrinal development under the Due Process Clause and the voting patterns on the Court therefore augured well for Earl Brewer as he appealed *Brown* v. *Mississippi* to the Court in the summer of 1935. Despite the divisions that were apparent on the court in other areas of constitutional law, there was a solid majority on the Court, cutting across factional lines among the justices, favoring the imposition of stricter procedural restrictions upon the conduct of state criminal trials under the Due Process Clause. And the *Snyder* case was evidence of how strict those standards had become by 1935, since the dissenters in that case, composed of representatives of all factions on the Court, had been only one vote shy of reversing a state criminal conviction on the comparatively technical ground involved in that case. Given the undenied brutality by which the confessions had been elicited in the *Brown* case, it could be predicted with relative confidence that a majority of the Court would find that the fundamental fairness required by the Due Process Clause had been denied Brown, Shields, and Ellington by the State of Mississippi.

The cause of the Kemper County trio was probably further enhanced by the fact that the coercion of confessions through "third-degree" methods had been widely publicized and condemned in the early 1930s. Two books on the third-degree methods of the nation's police forces, published in 1930 and 1931, received considerable public attention.[34] More important, the National Commission on Law Observance and Enforcement, popularly called the Wickersham Commission after its chairman, former attorney general George Wickersham, issued a report in 1931 based upon surveys of police practices in fifteen major cities that documented the widespread use of physical brutality and psychological coercion in eliciting confessions.[35] The nation was thus informed by a presidential commission that police brutality and third-degree methods of extracting confessions were apparently nationwide

problems. And the public awareness that the totalitarian re-
gimes in Communist Russia, Fascist Italy, and Nazi Germany
utilized police-state brutality as a method of governance undoubtedly heightened public sensitivity to the problem of the
use of similar tactics by American police.[36]

The climate of public opinion as well as doctrinal developments under the Due Process Clause therefore appeared to
favor Earl Brewer's contentions in his brief and oral argument
before the Supreme Court that coerced confessions should be
condemned under the Constitution. Brewer was assisted in
preparing his brief in *Brown* v. *Mississippi* by his young associate, William H. Hewitt, and fellow Jackson attorney J. Morgan
Stevens, whose wife Ethel Featherstun Stevens had been active
in the raising of funds for the appeal in Mississippi. The brief
on behalf of the Kemper County trio was finally completed
and filed in the Supreme Court on 2 January 1936, and it
bristled with indignation at the treatment Brown, Shields, and
Ellington had received at the hands of Mississippi officials and
courts.

Because of the Supreme Court's decision in *Twining* v.
New Jersey in 1908, [37] holding that the federal Constitution did
not guarantee a right against compulsory self-incrimination in
state proceedings, Brewer did not argue in the brief that the use
of coerced confessions as evidence against the Kemper trio
violated their right against self-incrimination. Relying upon
Mooney v. *Holohan*, however, he charged that the use of the
coerced confessions constituted a denial of the right to a fair
trial as secured by the Due Process Clause of the Fourteenth
Amendment. By introducing the coerced confessions at the
trial, Brewer argued, "the State of Mississippi offered evidence
essentially false and tainted further by the criminal manner in
which the statements were secured." "On the ground of fraud,
there is very little to choose between the act of the State,
referred to in *Mooney* v. *Holohan* . . .," he said, "and the act
of the State in the present case. The State of Mississippi,
through its use, as confessions, of statements literally whipped,
word for word, from petitioners, presented evidence as false as
perjury. The fraud in the two cases, as to the introduction of
false testimony, is essentially the same."[38]

"Why are these negroes sentenced to hang?" Brewer asked rhetorically. "Surely not for the murder of Raymond Stuart, for there is no competent evidence in the record against them on which a conviction for this crime could be based, but simply because their attorneys (who were appointed by the Court) failed to object to the extorted confessions in the proper form of words at precisely the proper stage of the proceedings. The Supreme Court of Mississippi based its affirmance of this case on the original appeal on the fact that counsel for petitioners did not move to exclude the admittedly incompetent confessions after their introduction." Could a mere error of procedure made by "indifferent counsel" thus validly result in the denial of the rights of the Kemper trio, Brewer asked the Court, "who, despite the fact they were ignorant, illiterate 'cornfield' negroes, took the stand (and not having legal training or being cognizant of technical rules of procedure) with all the earnestness of their souls, did all in their power to object and to move to exclude the illegal and incompetent . . . [evidence]?" "And all the time," Brewer continued, with "the negroes moving to exclude in the only way they knew how, their bodies were also pleading (the marks of the rope and lash were visible to all who gazed upon them) to the court not to allow these purported confessions, so brutally extorted, to be used against them"[39]

The State of Mississippi nevertheless contended, Brewer noted, that a formal motion must be made to exclude an illegally obtained confession; otherwise such a confession was still admissible as evidence under Mississippi procedure. "This seems to us to be quibbling of the utmost insincerity," he continued. "The whole defense in this case was based upon a denial of the legality of these confessions. The means by which they were extorted were laid bare before the Court and jury in all their hideousness. They were repeatedly objected to, but no precise motion to exclude was made. However, no one could have been deceived as to the wishes of the petitioners with respect to these so-called confessions." Yet the Supreme Court of Mississippi, by affirming the convictions of the Kemper trio, "attempts to defeat . . . [their] right . . . to a fair and impartial trial and this by a mere rule of procedure. A conviction thus obtained by illegal evidence is no triumph for justice and does not tend to uphold the majesty of the law."[40]

The Mississippi Supreme Court had thus held that Brown, Shields, and Ellington had waived their right to object to the confessions because their counsel had not objected to their admissibility as evidence at the trial, Brewer continued. But there had been an objection to the admissibility of the confessions when they were first introduced at the trial, Brewer argued, and in view of the fact that "the whole defense was predicated upon a denial of the truth of such statements, and an exposition [was made] of the shameful and hideous manner in which they were extorted, it is inconceivable to us that the doctrine of waiver is here correctly applied."[41]

But, "sweeping all argument as to waiver aside," Brewer declared, the State of Mississippi had "destroyed the validity of the trial" by denying the Kemper trio fundamental rights guaranteed under the Due Process Clause. "Because of the fraud of the State the binding effect of the whole proceeding against these petitioners was totally vitiated and destroyed; and under the circumstances the waiver of the petitioners, if it can properly be said that there was one, was of no more effect than the illegal and void proceedings which occurred prior thereto." "We submit, therefore," Brewer continued, "that it is apparent that any rule of procedure adopted by the Supreme Court of Mississippi, which serves as a device by which the court may ignore the denial in the lower court of those fundamentals essential to due process of law, is so arbitrary and unjustifiable a denial of essential justice, as to be within itself a denial of due process of law. And especially does this seem true in that the error of procedure was committed by counsel appointed by the court at a time and under circumstances, which made adequate representation impossible."[42]

The State of Mississippi was represented in the Supreme Court by William Dow Conn, Jr., and William H. Maynard, assistant attorneys general. On the coerced-confession issue, the state argued in the Supreme Court that while the Mississippi Constitution prohibited compulsory self-incrimination, that right had not been violated as far as the Kemper trio were concerned because the Mississippi Supreme Court had held that it had not been invoked with regard to the admission of the confessions at the trial. And the U.S. Supreme Court, the state noted, lacked any jurisdiction to reverse a state supreme court's interpretation of state law or the state constitution.[43]

As far as the federal Constitution was concerned, the state contended, under the Court's decision in *Twining* v. *New Jersey* there was no federal constitutional right against compulsory self-incrimination applicable in a state proceeding. The State of Mississippi therefore submitted "that there is nothing in the Federal Constitution which is infringed by the use in state courts of coerced confessions, even if we concede that the confessions in this case were so coerced; or, stated in other words, the exemption from compulsory self-incrimination in the courts of the States is not secured by any part of the Federal Constitution." The Self-Incrimination Clause of the Fifth Amendment of the federal Constitution, the state argued, "has been uniformly held by this court" as not intended "to limit the powers of the State Governments in respect to their own people, but to operate on the National Government alone. It regulates the procedure of the Federal Courts exclusively, and is not obligatory upon the several States of the Union."[44]

Since there was no federal constitutional right against compulsory self-incrimination, the use of the allegedly coerced confessions against the Kemper trio did not offend the federal Constitution in that regard, the state contended, and the only remaining question was whether the use of the confessions violated the Due Process Clause of the Fourteenth Amendment. The Due Process Clause, it was pointed out, merely guaranteed to criminal defendants in state proceedings the right to adequate notice of the charges against them and the opportunity of a fair hearing, and the states were left free to adopt their own procedural rules governing the conduct of their criminal trials. Mississippi, the state argued in its brief, had adopted a procedural rule that required the issue of the admissibility of confessions to be preliminarily considered by the trial court in the absence of the jury, and if the confession appeared to be free and voluntary, the trial judge could admit the confession as evidence to be considered by the jury. If, as the trial proceeded, testimony or evidence surfaced indicating that the confession had not been free and voluntary, counsel for the defense had to object to the confession's admissibility. Otherwise the confession could still be considered by the jury.

In the *Brown* case, the state argued, "the showing upon the preliminary inquiry into the competency of the confessions satisfied . . . [the court] that they were voluntary. There was nothing shown to the contrary by the prisoners or anyone else at this preliminary inquiry." "Afterwards," the state conceded, "when the prisoners were testifying on the merits of the case, they testified in such a way as to throw doubt upon the competency of their confessions, as related by state witnesses. But they never, from that time on, called upon the court by motion, or any other procedural step which required it to again rule upon the competency of this evidence in the light of the subsequent testimony. The Mississippi Supreme Court, in reviewing the trial, and in affirming the decision of the trial court, merely followed old, well established rules of practice and procedure, . . . and particularly the case of *Loftin* vs. *State.*"[45]

"The State of Mississippi is free to formulate and regulate its own forms or methods of procedure and practice," the state submitted; "it has done so; the petitioners have been tried according to well-settled and established rules and regulations governing trials of criminal cases; there has been no arbitrary action which denies to them any fundamental rights or which conflicts with a single specific provision of the Federal Constitution; and, consequently, 'due process of law,' as that [phrase] is used in the Fourteenth Amendment, has been accorded them."[46]

The Court's decision in *Mooney* v. *Holohan* did not apply to the facts in *Brown* v. *Mississippi*, the state further argued, since there was "no hint of perjury in the record before this court." The Kemper trio had admitted at the trial that they had told the witnesses for the state what those witnesses had testified to, the state noted. "No testimony was concealed from . . . [the defendants]. They knew better than anyone else, perhaps, just exactly what did happen, and they admit that the true circumstances are before the court. We are not dealing here with three innocent men, but three guilty ones, as clearly appears from their own cross-examinations. Not only this, but on the very day of the trial, two of them voluntarily called the Sheriff of the County aside and told him that they had told him the truth when they were in the Lauderdale County jail. Where is there any fraud? any deliberate deception?"[47]

The Court should also notice, the state said, that the confessions actually used at the trial were not the products of coercion. Earl Brewer "leaves the impression in his brief that the confessions which were used were the direct result of beatings administered by those who testified with reference to the confessions, but the record does not bear him out on that ground," the state asserted. "He further assumes that the wrongful influences used in obtaining the initial confessions still obtained when the later confessions were given. The petitioners' own testimony on cross-examination negatives any charge of force, threats, intimidation and the like, and not only shows that there was no abuse, ill-treatment or other form of coercion indulged in at the time, but on the other hand they say that they were kindly treated at this latter interview." The only explanation of why they confessed to the sheriffs of Kemper and Lauderdale counties offered by Brown, Shields, and Ellington, the state concluded, "is that they were 'scared,' and their version of the circumstances surrounding . . . [the later interviews with the sheriffs] shows that they were not 'scared,' but, that as they told . . . Sheriff . . . [Adcock] at the time of the trial, they told him the truth about what happened on the night of this brutal murder."[48]

In addition to attacking the state's use of the coerced confessions to convict the Kemper trio, Earl Brewer also relied upon the first Scottsboro case, *Powell* v. *Alabama*, as the basis of an alternative argument that Brown, Shields, and Ellington had been denied due process at their trial because they had been denied the effective assistance of counsel. "The right to a hearing as a basic element of due process has repeatedly been construed to include the right to the aid of counsel," Brewer pointed out to the Court. "This Court ruled very positively on this subject in the recent case of *Powell* v. *Alabama*. . . . The right to aid of counsel has been repeatedly held to be no mere form or ceremony, but a substantial right, and thus a Court is bound to make an effective appointment of counsel, taking into consideration all of the circumstances."[49]

John Clark and L. P. Spinks had been appointed counsel for Brown, Shields, and Ellington the day before the trial, and Joe H. Daws and D. P. Davis had been appointed as defense counsel on the day of the trial. According to Clark's affidavit filed in the Mississippi Supreme Court, there had been inadequate time to confer with the defendants and to prepare a defense. "In order to satisfy the requirement of due process of law, in view of the fact that these negroes are ignorant paupers, the trial court was under a positive duty of appointing them counsel at a time and under circumstances which would, in fact, allow the defense adequate preparation," Earl Brewer argued. "This the Court did not do. It is apparent that counsel for petitioners had no real opportunity to prepare for the trial of this cause. The element of time alone precluded them." "A careful study of the record in this case will reveal to any legal mind," he added, "that the attorneys representing the petitioners were only half-heartedly going through the empty form of a trial and were not in truth and in fact attempting to protect the rights of these defendants."[50]

Conn and Maynard, for the State, also disputed Brewer's argument on the right-to-counsel issue, pointing out that the Mississippi Supreme Court had concluded that the Kemper trio had been represented by "eminent counsel" at their trial. But in any case, the state argued, the right-to-counsel issue was "not raised in the trial court, and the State Supreme Court, the highest court of review in the State, has refused to consider it because of such fact [and] this court must likewise refuse to review this matter."[51]

The right-to-counsel issue under *Powell* v. *Alabama* was raised for the first time in the Mississippi Supreme Court, the state pointed out, when Earl Brewer filed a motion in arrest of judgment and for a new trial to which was attached John Clark's affidavit attesting to the inadequacy of the defense of the Kemper trio by counsel at their trial. "The filing of this pretended 'Motion to Arrest Judgment and For a New Trial,'" the state declared, "constitutes a palpable and deliberate, though abortive, attempt on the part of counsel to bring, by way of ex parte affidavits, the case within the decision of this court in *Powell* v. *Alabama.*" Such a motion, the state charged, "has absolutely no place in Mississippi procedure. The Mississippi Supreme Court refused to consider it because it was not properly a part of the record of the trial, and since that court could not consider it, neither can this court."[52]

In addition to these arguments contained in the briefs filed by both sides in the case, the Supreme Court scheduled oral argument in *Brown* v. *Mississippi* for 10 January 1936. This, however, created a problem for Earl Brewer, since he was scheduled to appear in federal court in New Orleans on January 9. The only possible way that he could appear in court in New Orleans on the 9th and still be in Washington to argue the *Brown* case on the 10th was to book a flight on an airline, but Brewer had never flown before and apparently viewed this prospect with some trepidation. "You won't go alone," Mrs. Brewer told her husband. "I'll go with you. Our children are grown, [and] if we have an accident we'll be together." It was therefore from the New Orleans airport that Earl Brewer, accompanied by his wife, sped by air to Washington to present to the Supreme Court his oral argument on behalf of Brown, Shields, and Ellington.[53]

Observers of the oral argument in the courtroom on 10 January reported to the NAACP that Brewer "made a very effective appeal and the members of the Supreme Court were visibly shocked at the story of the way the confessions were extorted from" the Kemper trio.[54] Brown, Shields, and Ellington had been forced to confess the killing of Raymond Stuart, Brewer told the Court, and they had been "cut to pieces with the buckles on the strap" that had been used to torture them. "There was not a bit of evidence offered at the trial [other than the coerced confessions]," he continued, "to sustain the indictment against them." And in a voice filled with emotion, Brewer declared to the Court that the Mississippi officials responsible for the torture of the Kemper trio had been "walking with the mob."[55]

Chief Justice Hughes, as well as Justices Sutherland, Roberts, Van Devanter, Stone, and Cardozo, directed pointed and hostile questions at Maynard and Conn during their oral presentation of the state's case. The question raised by the case, Chief Justice Hughes told counsel for the state, appeared to be whether there had been "a denial of the fundamental conception of justice," and the other justices commented sharply on what appeared to be "torture whippings" and "extorted confessions." William Conn argued nevertheless that the Court was not presented with a valid federal question in the case, but Justice Cardozo interrupted to point out that the Court had never held that the torture of accused persons by state officers was not open for review. And Justice Stone observed that the record showed "the men had been maltreated physically in the presence of state officers."[56]

William Maynard, however, pointed out that there had been no motion to exclude the confessions at the trial as required by Mississippi procedure, but he too was interrupted by one of the justices. Should Brown, Shields, and Ellington be condemned to die "because their lawyer neglected to say, 'I object'?" the justice asked Maynard. Maynard was speechless in the face of the question, feeling that if he replied in the negative, he would be conceding his case, while if he answered "yes" to the question, he would appear to be heartless. Maynard instead of answering dropped his head in silence, and the justice said, "I thought so."[57]

The difficult time Conn and Maynard had with the Court during the oral argument "prompted the belief among observers," the Jackson *Daily Clarion-Ledger* reported, "that the Supreme Court would order a new trial for Ed Brown, Henry Shields and Yank Ellington."[58] And in an editorial two days after the oral argument in the *Brown* case, the *Clarion-Ledger* once again gave voice to the nervousness the Mississippi press had previously expressed regarding the proceedings affecting the Kemper trio. A new trial for the Kemper County trio, the *Clarion-Ledger* said, would "be welcomed by many Mississippians who not only want justice done but who realize how closely this case parallels the notorious 'Scottsboro case' of Alabama and how damaging it could be to Mississippi." "The records show that confessions were obtained from the three negroes by torture," the newspaper noted. "The State, not denying this when the case was before the State Supreme Court on appeal, merely contended that attorneys for the negroes failed to move at the proper time to exclude the confessions because of the manner in which they were obtained, and that the convictions therefore should not be set aside on these grounds."[59]

The Mississippi Supreme Court had sustained the state's argument, the *Clarion-Ledger* continued, but Judges Griffith and Anderson had vigorously dissented "in language that aroused national interest." "Many thoughtful and justice-loving Mississippians would welcome a decision, under these conditions," the newspaper concluded, "giving the three a new trial. If they are guilty, it can be proved and punishment meted. If they are not guilty and these torture-obtained confessions are false, then decent Mississippians don't want to see the three hanged."[60]

While Earl Brewer appeared to be the consensus victor in the oral argument in *Brown* v. *Mississippi,* the publicity given the case by the *Clarion-Ledger* was not matched by the press generally. Just as the Supreme Court's confrontation with the New Deal had overshadowed the appeal of the *Brown* case to the Court, it was also the fate of the *Brown* case to be largely overlooked as it was pending decision because the focus of attention of the national media was upon the question of the constitutionality of the Tennessee Valley Authority. One of the New Deal's more controversial programs, the TVA sought to initiate governmentally controlled generation and sale of electricity throughout the Tennessee Valley region, ousting the private utility companies in the area, but the TVA's constitutional validity had been challenged before the Supreme Court in *Ashwander* v. *TVA.*[61] The *Ashwander* case was argued before the Court on 19 and 20 December 1935, but it remained undecided by the Court as the *Brown* case was argued orally, and the focus of attention of the national media was upon the fate of the TVA and how the Court's decision in the *Ashwander* case would affect its continuing confrontation with the New Deal.

As it turned out, the opinions of the Court in both *Brown* v. *Mississippi* and *Ashwander* v. *TVA* were announced on 17

February 1936, with the result that the *Brown* decision was largely buried by the publicity surrounding the Court's decision upholding the validity of the TVA in the *Ashwander* case.[62] As *Time* reported the events of 17 February, when Chief Justice Hughes and his colleagues parted the red velvet curtains behind the Supreme Court bench promptly at noon, "U.S. Supreme Court addicts were sure that after being disappointed for a month they were at last going to be rewarded with a decision on the Tennessee Valley Authority." Word had leaked out that the Supreme Court police had been advised to eat lunch early because the session of the Court would be a long one. And reporters who spotted Mrs. Charles Evans Hughes in the courtroom audience knew that the chief justice often alerted his wife when the Court was to deliver a particularly important decision.[63]

The chief justice began to read an opinion, but after "the first sentence, the crowd sighed," since it was obvious that the opinion being read did not deal with the TVA. "Even the deepest-dyed Liberal," *Time* said, "hardly gave a hoot that day about Brown *et al.* v. State of Mississippi—three Negroes convicted of murder, whose statements, claimed to have been made when they were brutally whipped by deputy sheriffs, were admitted in evidence as confessions." "The Chief Justice of the U.S. was not disinterested," *Time* noted, and he proceeded to read the unanimous opinion of the Court in the *Brown* case, reversing the convictions of the Kemper County trio. "Having contributed to the dramatic tension by putting human rights first," *Time* said, "Chief Justice Hughes took up property rights next," and then read the Court's opinion upholding the TVA in the *Ashwander* case.[64]

Given the fact that the Kemper trio had rather clearly not received the effective assistance of counsel at their trial, the Supreme Court could have decided the *Brown* case on the right-to-counsel issue. If this had occurred, the *Brown* case would have been virtually indistinguishable from the Court's 1932 decision in the first Scottsboro case, *Powell v. Alabama*, and as such, the *Brown* case would have lost most of its significance. However, Chief Justice Hughes and a unanimous Court opted to base the decision in *Brown* v. *Mississippi* squarely upon the issue of the coerced confessions, with the consequence that the Court for the first time not only reversed a state conviction because of the use of coerced confessions against the defendants, but also significantly expanded the meaning of the fair-trial rule under the Due Process Clause of the Fourteenth Amendment.

"The question in this case is whether convictions, which rest solely upon confessions shown to have been extorted by officers of the State by brutality and violence," Chief Justice Hughes thus opened the opinion in the *Brown* case, "are consistent with the due process of law required by the Fourteenth Amendment of the Constitution of the United States." Brown, Shields, and Ellington, the chief justice continued, "were indicted for the murder of one Raymond [Stuart], whose death occurred on March 30, 1934. They were indicted on April 4, 1934, and were then arraigned and pleaded not guilty. Counsel were appointed by the court to defend them. Trial was begun the next morning and was concluded on the following day, when they were found guilty and sentenced to death." "Aside from the confessions, there was no evidence to warrant the submission of the case to the jury," Hughes pointed out. "After a preliminary inquiry, testimony as to the confessions was received over the objection by defendants' counsel. Defendants then testified that the confessions were false and had been procured by physical torture. The case went to the jury with instructions, upon request of defendants' counsel, that if the jury had reasonable doubt as to the confessions having resulted from coercion, and that they were not true, they were not to be considered as evidence."[65]

Following their convictions, the defendants appealed to the Mississippi Supreme Court, Hughes noted, but the court affirmed the convictions although the admission of the confessions had been assigned as an error. Following the first decision of the Mississippi Supreme Court, both a motion in arrest of judgment and for a new trial, as well as a suggestion of error, were filed with the court. The motion in arrest of judgment and for a new trial had alleged, Hughes noted, that the evidence against the defendants had been "obtained by coercion and brutality known to the court and to the district attorney, and that the defendants had been denied the benefit of counsel or opportunity to confer with counsel in a reasonable manner." And the suggestion of error had challenged the "proceedings of the trial, in the use of the confessions and with respect to the alleged denial of representation by counsel, as violating the due process clause of the Fourteenth Amendment of the Constitution of the United States."[66]

The Mississippi Supreme Court, the chief justice continued, "entertained the suggestion of error, considered the federal question, and decided it against defendants' contentions." The grounds for the state supreme court's decision were that the right against compulsory self-incrimination was not a part of due process of law, and "that the failure of the trial court to exclude the confessions after the introduction of evidence showing their incompetency, in the absence of a request for such exclusion, did not deprive the defendants of life or liberty without due process of law; and that even if the trial court had erroneously overruled a motion to exclude the confessions, the ruling would have been mere error reversible on appeal, but not a violation of constitutional right."[67]

The majority opinion of the Mississippi Supreme Court had not "set forth the evidence as to the circumstances in which the confessions were procured," Hughes noted, but that the "evidence established that they were procured by coercion was not questioned." Indeed, he noted that the majority of the Mississippi Supreme Court had conceded that the testimony of the defendants at the trial indicated "that the confessions were not made voluntarily but were coerced." At this point in his opinion, the chief justice undoubtedly decided that the dissenting opinion of Judge Virgil Griffith in the Mississippi Supreme Court condemned the proceedings involving the Kemper trio as eloquently as anything he himself could say, and he therefore included Griffith's dissent almost in its entirety as a part of the opinion of the Court. "There is no dispute as to the facts [regarding the coercion of the confessions]," Hughes said, "and as they are clearly and adequately stated in the dissenting opinion of Judge Griffith (with whom Judge Anderson concurred)—showing both the extreme brutality of the measures to extort the confessions and the participation of the state authorities—we quote this part of his opinion in full. . . ."[68]

In his dissenting opinion in the Mississippi Supreme

Court, Judge Griffith had in effect called upon the U.S. Supreme Court to reverse the decision of his own court in the *Brown* case by pointing out that if "this judgment be affirmed by the Federal Supreme Court, it will be the first in the history of that court wherein was allowed to stand a conviction based solely upon testimony coerced by the barbarities of executive officers of the state, known to the prosecuting officers of the state as having been so coerced, when the testimony was introduced, and fully shown in all its nakedness to the trial judge before he closed the case and submitted it to the jury, and when all this is not only undisputed, but is expressly and openly admitted."[69] Now, much of Griffith's dissent became a substantial part of the opinion in which the U.S. Supreme Court accepted his invitation to reverse the decision of the state court. Griffith's graphic description of the brutality to which Brown, Shields, and Ellington had been subjected was quoted by Chief Justice Hughes, as well as his declaration that in "pertinent respects the transcript reads more like pages torn from some medieval account, than a record made within the confines of a modern civilization which aspires to an enlightened constitutional government."[70]

After his extensive quotation of Judge Griffith, Chief Justice Hughes turned to the State of Mississippi's argument that even if the confessions of the Kemper trio had been coerced, there could be no violation of the federal Constitution by their admission as evidence at the trial, since the Constitution did not guarantee a right against compulsory self-incrimination in a state proceeding under the Court's decision in *Twining* v. *New Jersey*. "But," Hughes said, "the question of the right of the State to withdraw the privilege against self-incrimination is not here involved." Statements in the *Twining* case and similar cases in which the Court had held that the states need not recognize the right against self-incrimination, he pointed out, referred to "the process of justice by which the accused may be called as a witness and required to testify. Compulsion by torture to extort a confession is a different matter."[71]

"The State is free to regulate the procedure of its courts in accordance with its own conceptions of policy, unless in so doing it 'offends some principle of justice so rooted in the traditions and conscience of our people as to be ranked as fundamental,' " Hughes continued. "The State may abolish trial by jury. It may dispense with indictment by grand jury and substitute complaint or information. . . . But the freedom of the State in establishing its policy is the freedom of constitutional government and is limited by the requirement of due process of law. Because a State may dispense with a jury trial, it does not follow that it may substitute trial by ordeal. The rack and torture chamber may not be substituted for the witness stand."[72]

Under the Court's decisions in *Moore* v. *Dempsey, Powell* v. *Alabama,* and *Mooney* v. *Holohan,* Hughes pointed out, the states could not permit mob dominated trials, deny counsel to indigent defendants in capital cases, or knowingly use perjured testimony to secure convictions without violating the Due Process Clause of the Fourteenth Amendment. "And the trial equally is a mere pretense where the state authorities have contrived a conviction resting solely upon confessions obtained by violence," Hughes declared. "The due process clause requires 'that state action, whether through one agency or another, shall be consistent with the fundamental principles of liberty and justice which lie at the base of all our civil and political institutions. . . .' It would be difficult to conceive of methods more revolting to the sense of justice than those taken to procure the confessions of these petitioners, and the use of the confessions thus obtained as the basis for conviction and sentence was a clear denial of due process."[73]

The State of Mississippi nevertheless maintained, the chief justice noted, that the confessions were properly admitted at the trial because counsel for the defendants failed to object to their use as evidence after it appeared that they were the products of coercion. This contention, Hughes declared, "proceeds upon a misconception of the nature of petitioners' complaint. That complaint is not of the commission of mere error, but of a wrong so fundamental that it made the whole proceeding a mere pretence of a trial and rendered the conviction and sentence wholly void. . . . We are not concerned with a mere question of state practice, or whether counsel assigned to petitioners were competent or mistakenly assumed that their first objections were sufficient."[74]

"In the instant case, the trial court was fully advised by the undisputed evidence of the way in which the confessions had been procured," Hughes continued. "The trial court knew that there was no other evidence upon which conviction and sentence could be based. Yet it proceeded to permit conviction and to pronounce sentence. The conviction and sentence were void for want of the essential element of due process, and the proceeding thus vitiated could be challenged in any appropriate manner." "It was challenged before the Supreme Court of the State by express invocation of the Fourteenth Amendment," Hughes concluded. "That court entertained the challenge, considered the federal question thus presented, but declined to enforce petitioners' constitutional right. The court thus denied a federal right fully established, and specially set up and claimed and the judgment must be reversed."[75]

Earl Brewer had therefore won the most sweeping victory possible in the Court, having convinced not just a majority but all of the justices that the use of the coerced confessions in the *Brown* case violated the Due Process Clause. And with the reversal of the convictions of the Kemper County trio, it appeared virtually certain that the gallows that had been constructed in the jail yard at DeKalb in the spring of 1934 would now go unused. More than geographical distance separated the marble palace of the Supreme Court in Washington and Kemper County, Mississippi, however. Despite the sweeping victory in the Court, Earl Brewer and the Kemper trio soon discovered that the fight to save their lives was not over.

1. Alpheus T. Mason, *William Howard Taft: Chief Justice* (New York: Simon and Schuster, 1964), pp. 133–37; Merlo J. Pusey, *Charles Evans Hughes*, 2 vols. (New York: Macmillan, 1952), 2:688–90.

2. Alpheus T. Mason, *Harlan Fiske Stone* (New York: Viking, 1956), pp. 405–6.

3. Oliver Wendell Holmes, Jr., "Law and the Court," reprinted in Alan F. Westin (ed.), *An Autobiography of the Supreme Court* (New York: Macmillan, 1963). p. 135.

4. Henry F. Pringle, *The Life and Times of William Howard Taft*, 2 vols. (New York: Farrar & Rinehard, 1939), 2:1044.

5. See Glendon A. Schubert, *Constitutional Politics* (New York: Holt, Rinehart and Winston, 1960), pp. 159–71.

6. There is, unfortunately, only one good biography regarding the members of the conservative bloc during the 1930s; it is Joel Francis Paschal, *Mr. Justice Sutherland: A Man against the State* (Princeton, N.J.: Princeton University Press, 1951). Unpublished materials on the "four horsemen" include Ronald F. Howell, "Conservative Influence on Constitutional Development, 1923–1937: The Constitutional Theory of Justices Van Devanter, McReynolds, Sutherland and Butler" (Baltimore, Md.: Ph.D. diss., Johns Hopkins University, 1952); and Doris Arlene Blaisdell, "The Constitutional Law of Mr. Justice McReynolds" (Madison: Ph.D. diss. University of Wisconsin, 1952). See also Earnest Sutherland Bates, "The Diehard Justices," *New Republic* 87 (17 June 1936): 166. An excellent analysis of the politics of judicial selection involving the appointment of Pierce Butler to the Court during the Taft court years may also be found in David J. Danelski, *A Supreme Court Justice Is Appointed* (New York: Random House, 1964). Merlo J. Pusey, *Charles Evans Hughes* (New York: Macmillan, 1952), is the standard—albeit rather uncritical—biography of Hughes, while Owen Roberts's judicial performance is analyzed in Charles A. Leonard, *A Search for a Judicial Philosophy: Mr. Justice Roberts and the Constitutional Revolution of 1937* (Port Washington, N.Y.: Kennikat Press, 1971). The standard work on Brandeis is Alpheus T. Mason, *Brandeis: A Free Man's Life* (New York: Viking Press, 1946), but an intriguing recent analysis of Brandeis's extrajudicial activities may be found in Bruce Allen Murphy, *The Brandeis/Frankfurter Connection* (New York: Oxford University Press, 1982). Alpheus T. Mason, *Harlan Fiske Stone* (New York: Viking, 1956), is not only the authoritative biography of Stone but a classic of judicial biography. Unfortunately, Benjamin Cardozo has not received such classic treatment; George S. Hellman, *Benjamin N. Cardozo: American Judge* (New York: McGraw-Hill, 1940), at least furnishes the basic facts of Cardozo's life.

7. *Literary Digest* 121 (22 Feb. 1936): 5.

8. *Nation* 142 (15 Jan. 1936): 61.

9. Barron v. Baltimore, 7 Pet. 243 (U.S. 1833).

10. Hurtado v. California, 110 U.S. 516 (1884). For an analysis of the *Hurtado* case, see Richard C. Cortner, *The Supreme Court and the Second Bill of Rights* (Madison: University of Wisconsin Press, 1981), pp. 12–22.

11. Twining v. New Jersey, 211 U.S. 78, 105–6, 110–14 (1908). The accuracy of the Court's historical analysis in the *Twining* case has been seriously questioned. See Leonard W. Levy, *Origins of the Fifth Amendment* (New York: Oxford University Press, 1968), preface and

pp. 334–35. For an analysis of the *Twining* case, see Cortner, *Supreme Court and Second Bill of Rights*, pp. 38–49.

12. 211 U.S. 78, 99, 97–106.

13. Gitlow v. New York, 268 U.S. 652, 665–66 (1925).

14. Stromberg v. California, 283 U.S. 359 (1931).

15. Near v. Minnesota, 283 U.S. 697 (1931). See also Cortner, *Supreme Court and Second Bill of Rights*, pp. 50–87. On the *Near* case, see Fred W. Friendly, *Minnesota Rag* (New York: Random House, 1981).

16. Grosjean v. American Press Co., 297 U.S. 233, 244 (1936).

17. Maxwell v. Dow, 176 U.S. 581 (1900).

18. In re Kemmler, 136 U.S. 436 (1890); McElvaine v. Bush, 142 U.S. 155 (1891); O'Neil v. Vermont, 144 U.S. 323 (1892).

19. West v. Louisiana, 197 U.S. 258 (1904).

20. Spies v. Illinois, 123 U.S. 131 (1887).

21. Frank v. Mangum, 237 U.S. 309 (1915). On the *Frank* case, see Leonard Dinnerstein, *The Leo Frank Case* (New York: Columbia University Press, 1968).

22. Moore v. Dempsey, 261 U.S. 86 (1923).

23. Ibid., p. 91.

24. Tumey v. Ohio, 273 U.S. 510 (1927).

25. Powell v. Alabama, 287 U.S. 45 (1932).

26. Mooney v. Holohan, 293 U.S. 103, 112 (1935).

27. See Cortner, *Supreme Court and Second Bill of Rights*, pp. 124–51.

28. Ibid., p. 288.

29. 261 U.S. 86, 92–102.

30. 287 U.S. 45, 73–77.

31. See J. Woodford Howard, "On the Fluidity of Judicial Choice," *American Political Science Review* 62 (March 1968): 43–56.

32. Snyder v. Massachusetts, 291 U.S. 97 (1934).

33. Ibid., pp. 102–22, 123–38.

34. Emanuel H. Lavine, *The "Third Degree": A Detailed and Appalling Exposé of Police Brutality* (New York: Vanguard Press, 1930); Ernest J. Hopkins, *Our Lawless Police* (New York: Viking, 1931). See also Otis H. Stephens, *The Supreme Court and Confessions of Guilt* (Knoxville: University of Tennessee Press, 1973), pp. 39–40.

35. National Commission on Law Observance and Enforcement, *Report on Lawlessness in Law Enforcement* (Washington, D.C.: U.S. Government Printing Office, 1931).

36. Stephens, *Supreme Court and Confessions*, p. 41.

37. Twining v. New Jersey, 211 U.S. 78 (1908).

38. Statement and Brief for Petitioners, Record, *Brown v. Mississippi*, p. 21.

39. Ibid., p. 34.

40. Ibid., p. 35.

41. Ibid., pp. 35–36.

42. Ibid., pp. 36–37.

43. Brief of Respondent, ibid., pp. 3–4.

44. Ibid., pp. 4–5.

45. Ibid., p. 21.

46. Ibid., p. 29.

47. Ibid., pp. 63–64.

48. Ibid., pp. 64–65.

49. Statement and Brief for Petitioners, ibid., p. 23.

50. Ibid., p. 24.

51. Brief of Respondent, ibid., p. 35.

52. Ibid., p. 46. In his brief, Earl Brewer additionally argued that the trial court had lost jurisdiction because of the violations of due process at the trial (Statement and Brief for Petitioners, ibid., pp. 25–26) and that due process was also violated because the Kemper trio had not been afforded an opportunity to file a motion for a new trial in the trial court (Statement and Brief for Petitioners, ibid., pp. 30–33). These points were of course disputed by the state (Brief of Respondent, ibid., pp. 47–63), but because the coerced-confession and right-to-counsel issues were the principal issues raised before the Court, I have not dealt with these subsidiary issues.

53. Letter from Claudia Brewer Strite to author, 18 July 1981.

54. Memorandum for Mr. Wilkins on Cases for the Board Report, 4 Feb. 1936, NAACP Papers, D–12; see also *Crisis* 43 (Feb. 1936): 59.

55. Jackson *Daily Clarion-Ledger*, 11 Jan. 1936, p. 1.

56. Ibid., pp. 1, 3.

57. Letter from Claudia Brewer Strite to author, 18 July 1981.

58. Jackson *Daily Clarion-Ledger*, 11 Jan. 1936, p. 1.

59. Ibid., 12 Jan. 1936, p. 6, editorial, "A New Trial for These Three Would Be Welcome in Mississippi."

60. Ibid.

61. Ashwander v. TVA, 297 U.S. 288 (1936).

62. A good example of the press coverage regarding the two cases was the coverage in the Washington *Star* and the Washington *Post*. The *Star* ran extensive coverage of the *Ashwander* decision on page 1, but failed to mention the *Brown* decision. The *Post* also covered the *Ashwander* decision on page 1, but ran only a brief report of the *Brown* case on page 7. See Washington *Star*, 17 Feb. 1936, pp. 1, 7; Washington *Post*, 18 Feb. 1936, pp. 1, 7.

63. *Time* 27 (24 Feb. 1936): 6.

64. Ibid.

65. Brown v. Mississippi, 297 U.S. 278, 279 (1936).

66. Ibid., p. 280.

67. Ibid.

68. Ibid., pp. 280–81.
69. Brown v. State, 178 Miss. 563, 574 (1935).
70. 297 U.S. 278, 281–85.
71. Ibid., p. 285.
72. Ibid., p. 286.
73. Ibid.
74. Ibid., pp. 286–87
75. Ibid., p. 287.

7

Brown v. Mississippi
Remand and Aftermath

When the United States Supreme Court announced its decision in *Brown* v. *Mississippi* in February 1936, *Time* magazine accurately reported that the decision of the case of the Kemper trio was overshadowed by the Court's decisions concerning questions of economic policy raised by the New Deal. It was therefore not unexpected that the press reactions to the Court's decision in the *Brown* case were largely in the context of the increased likelihood of a serious confrontation between the Court and President Roosevelt and the New Deal. And since the press was overwhelmingly opposed to the New Deal, the *Brown* decision was cited by the press as evidence of the value of the Court in the governmental system, and the decision was used as ammunition for editorial denunciations of proposals to curb the power of the Court that were being increasingly discussed.

The *New York Times*, for example, declared editorially that in the *Brown* decision, "the Supreme Court once more appears in the aspect usually overlooked by those excited radicals who see it only as a set of 'nine old obstructionists.'" In the *Brown* case, as in the Scottsboro cases, the *Times* said, "the court stands as the protector of . . . a fair trial, and other individual liberties. It 'obstructs,' indeed, but what it obstructs is injustice, brutality and tyranny."[1]

The Washington *Post* responded to the *Brown* decision in a similar vein, acknowledging editorially that public interest "in the so-called TVA decision unfortunately obscured the equally important opinion in which the Supreme Court on Monday scathingly denounced the use of 'third degree' methods. No decision in recent years has been more pointed or emphatic in its demand for observance of the human rights guaranteed to every citizen by the fundamental law." The method by which confessions had been obtained from Brown, Shields, and Ellington, the *Post* declared, constituted a "despicable reversion to savagery." "Those who feel it desirable to curb the appellate powers of the Supreme Court may well give heed to this opinion," the *Post* continued. "Had the court been denied the power of judicial review, these Negroes, against whom no legitimate evidence has been presented, would have been executed." The Court, the *Post* concluded, "stands as a bulwark of human as well as property rights. To weaken it in one sphere would be to lessen its efficacy in the other."[2]

It was, however, the Chicago *Tribune*, which under the direction of Colonel Robert R. (Bertie) McCormick was one of the most vociferous opponents of the New Deal, that responded most dramatically to the decision in *Brown v. Mississippi*. On 15 March, almost a month after the Supreme Court's decision, the *Tribune* published a two-page editorial account of the proceedings regarding the Kemper County trio, including a complete reprinting of the opinion of Chief Justice Hughes in the case. "Mississippi Justice, U.S. Supreme Court Upsets Trial by Rack and Lash," and "The Supreme Court's Challenge to the State of Mississippi," were the headlines introducing the *Tribune's* material on the *Brown* case. "For those inclined to look upon opinions by the United States Supreme Court as dry and colorless documents there is a thrilling surprise in store in a decision handed down recently by that body," the *Tribune* said. "The opinion has to do with a murder in a backwoods region in Mississippi. It reveals a story of stark terror, torture, and brutality that eclipses even the horror tales of the middle ages. The rope and the lash are exposed as having taken the place of justice in a part of the land ordinarily believed to be inhabited by civilized people." "For those who would wish to curb the powers of this highest tribunal of the nation," the *Tribune* declared, echoing the *New York Times* and Washington *Post,* "there is a profound lesson in the opinion rendered in the Mississippi murder case."[3]

The St. Louis *Post-Dispatch* also editorially contrasted the Court's decision in the *Ashwander* and *Brown* cases, pointing out that the Court had "upheld the rights of three humble citizens under the Constitution," while rejecting a challenge to the TVA. "Is any more proof needed," the *Post-Dispatch* asked, "to refute the subversive suggestions that the court is concerned only with protecting the interest of 'big business'?"[4]

The most outraged press reaction to the torture inflicted upon Brown, Shields, and Ellington came from the black-operated *Chicago Defender.* The Supreme Court's opinion, the *Chicago Defender* declared, "clearly indicates to what depth of putridity, prejudice and hate the lower court of Mississippi has sunk." "It is not quite clear to people who live in intelligent communities how members of the 'presumed superior race' can fall so low in the depths of judicial depravity," the newspaper continued. "It would appear that the courts themselves would have greater respect for what the world thinks of their decisions than to surrender their judicial integrity to prejudice. The judge, prosecuting attorney and the sheriff knew that the three defendants were being convicted on false testimony; yet the whole judicial system and law enforcing agencies of the state gave the full power of their various offices to the conviction."[5]

The *Nation* had of course given national publicity to the *Brown* case prior to the Court's decision, and, although it continued to be highly critical of the Court's decisions invalidating New Deal programs, the publication responded favorably to the Court's decision in the *Brown* case. "The processes of justice work so slowly for Negroes that if justice is ever won by them it is more a matter of miracles than of retribution," the *Nation* said. And in the *Brown* case, there had been "a whole succession of miracles." The first miracle had been the appointment of John Clark as defense counsel, "a very able and humane white Southerner . . ., who set for himself the task of compensating by his own humanity and energy for all the wrongs which his fellow-whites had inflicted on the Negroes." "The second miracle," the *Nation* continued, "was Associate Justice Griffith of the Mississippi Supreme Court, who, even when the majority had denied the appeal of the . . . [Kemper trio] from the conviction, read a magnificent dissenting opinion in which the entire story of the torture of the defendants and the forced confessions was set down." "The climax of the case has now come," the *Nation* said, "in an opinion by Chief Justice Hughes in which he sets aside the convictions. The editors of *The Nation* are proud to have printed an article in the issue of December 1, 1935, . . . which told the story and helped arouse interest in the case."[6]

In contrast to the rather widespread editorial comments on the *Brown* decision in the Northern press, most of the leading Southern newspapers did not comment on the case.[7] Two Southern newspapers that did have editorial reactions to the case, the Chattanooga *Daily Times* and the Memphis *Commercial Appeal*, reflected very different views regarding the decision. The *Daily Times* declared that the Supreme Court's opinion revealed a "shocking picture" of justice in Mississippi. "Civilized southerners, with pride in their section of the United States, have stoutly resisted depictions of the south which were written in terms of ignorance and cruelty," the *Daily Times* noted. "Lately the works of Erskine Caldwell—the play 'Tobacco Road' and the novel 'God's Little Acre'—have provoked indignant protests that they misrepresented the south. Whether the outcry against Mr. Caldwell is justified or not, the family of Jeeter Lister in 'Tobacco Road' and the family of Ty Ty Walden in 'God's Little Acre' could not, combined, afford a picture of more primitive barbarity than that of real life which was written into the record . . . by the Supreme Court." The Court's opinion, the *Daily Times* declared, was "a tacit indictment of a state's practice in the administration of law" and stopped "little short of a rebuke to the Mississippi Supreme Court." "The Southern mob has been a rank sore that is yielding bit by bit to the cure of light," the newspaper concluded. "The mob spirit and the mob methods in the Mississippi case which the Supreme Court of the United

States denounces, in language almost impassioned, are the more sinister because they exist under the cloak of justice."[8]

The Memphis *Commercial Appeal,* on the other hand, only backhandedly admitted the propriety of the Supreme Court's decision concerning the Kemper trio. Mississippi, the newspaper said, had extended the Court a "direct invitation for a first class wallop," and the result of the "invitation was just such a wallop, with the consequent threat throughout the country of the time-worn, unfair and dishonest criticism of southern justice which agitators and busybodies never let up on." "Prosecuting officers too often in their zeal bring on impossible situations," the *Commercial Appeal* continued. "It is too much like baiting the higher courts. The Scottsboro cases in Alabama have just about reached such a point. Of course it is popular nowadays for lawyers, without any other defense, to charge brutality and coercion when legal, free and voluntary confessions of criminals are involved. But judges and juries are generally able to determine the merits of such a plea." Nevertheless, the *Commercial Appeal* somewhat grudgingly admitted, the "Mississippi case will not redound to the credit of Mississippi justice."[9]

In Mississippi itself, there was no editorial comment on the *Brown* decision by the Meridian *Star,* although the *Star* had editorially praised the original trial of Brown, Shields, and Ellington as being fair and conforming to due process of law. However, both the Jackson newspapers—the *Daily Clarion-Ledger* and the *Daily News* did comment on the decision: Both newspapers supported the Supreme Court's action. The *Daily News* editorialized that some "fairly good ideas do emanate from the minds of those 'Nine Old Meanies' who constitute our Supreme Court now sitting in Washington. They held last Monday, in a case, carried from Kemper county, Miss., that confessions of crime should not be whipped from human beings, even if they are black as the ace of spades." There had not been "a bit of first-hand or eye-witness evidence against" the Kemper trio, the *Daily News* said, "not even good circumstantial testimony. They were whipped until they confessed. Third degree stuff and almost as bad as the murder. The United

States Supreme Court decides that must not be done. The United States Supreme Court does decide right sometimes."[10]

The Jackson *Daily Clarion-Ledger,* on the other hand, continued to express anxiety over the effect the *Brown* case was having on Mississippi's national image. "The United States Supreme Court, in an eloquent decision which was bad advertising for Mississippi, sets aside the death sentences imposed upon three Kemper negroes for murder, holding that aside from confessions obtained by torture there was no evidence against the three sufficient to warrant submission of the case to a jury," the *Clarion-Ledger* said. "It is sufficient to quote one paragraph of the decision to illustrate how and why it was bad publicity for Mississippi. 'It would be difficult to conceive of methods more revolting to the sense of justice than those taken to procure the confessions of these petitioners. . . .'" "This decision is no more eloquently condemnatory than the minority opinion of the Mississippi Supreme Court on the same case written by Judge Griffith and concurred in by Judge Anderson," the *Clarion-Ledger* noted. "That minority opinion was also given national publicity, but since it was a Mississippi jurist's opinion on a Mississippi matter the publicity was not as costly to the state as that which is given this federal court decision."[11]

For Ed Brown, Henry Shields, and Yank Ellington the press reaction to the decision in their case was unimportant. What was important was the fact that with the Court's decision in *Brown* v. *Mississippi,* for the first time in almost two years the trio did not face the grim prospect of death by hanging in the jail yard in DeKalb. And for Earl Brewer and his colleagues, the decision could not have been a more complete vindication of their constitutional challenge to the convictions of the Kemper trio. Brewer visited the Hinds County jail in Jackson on 18 February and informed Brown, Shields, and Ellington of the Supreme Court's decision, assuring them that "freedom is in sight." "God bless you guvner," the trio shouted, and they reportedly spent the day singing black spirituals and praising God for the Supreme Court's decision.[12]

Interviewed by the press, Earl Brewer said he would not know what the next step in the case would be until he saw the formal decree of the Supreme Court and determined whether the Court ordered the Mississippi Supreme Court to release the Kemper trio or remanded the case for a new trial. "In any event, there is little likelihood that the negroes will be convicted again," Brewer said. "The conviction in the first instance was based solely upon the confessions of the negroes, and as the Supreme Court has ruled that these confessions, obtained by force, cannot be admitted as evidence, it seems certain that no further prosecution of the cases is to be expected."[13]

The NAACP was of course elated over Earl Brewer's victory in the Supreme Court, and the association noted that Brewer expected that the "state may dismiss the charges against the men."[14] "Outstanding in the Association's legal work has been its defense of Ed Brown, Yank Ellington and Henry Shields, three Negro sharecroppers in Mississippi," the NAACP reported. And ignoring the contributions of the Commission on Interracial Cooperation and Mississippi sources, the association claimed that it had "financed the entire fight, including the argument in the United States Supreme Court, at what we believe to be a record low cost. . . ." [15]

In contrast to the optimism of the NAACP and defense counsel regarding the final disposition of the *Brown* case, the black-operated *Chicago Defender* had warned after the Supreme Court's decision that the Court's action "in no way guarantees the freedom of the oppressed defendants as the case must be returned to Mississippi courts where feeling against the men is high for retrial."[16] The *Chicago Defender's* warning proved to be prescient, since the NAACP and defense counsel had not anticipated the grim determination of District Attorney John Stennis to punish Brown, Shields, and Ellington, and it was Stennis who would ultimately have the power to dismiss the charges or to retry the Kemper trio.

After the U.S. Supreme Court's decision in the *Brown* case, Earl Brewer filed a motion in the Mississippi Supreme Court requesting that the Kemper trio be discharged from custody. However, in mid-April 1936, the state supreme court entered a judgment reversing the convictions of the trio but remanding the case to the Circuit Court of the Sixteenth Judicial District in Kemper County, for retrial. "In obedience to the mandate" of the U.S. Supreme Court, the state supreme court said, "the judgment of the court below will be reversed and the cause remanded for further proceedings not inconsistent with that opinion."[17] Although he had maintained an official silence regarding the decision of the U.S. Supreme Court, District Attorney John Stennis had indicated that he would seek a retrial of the case, much to the consternation of the NAACP, the Commission on Interracial Cooperation, defense counsel, and presumably Brown, Shields, and Ellington themselves.[18]

"Of course, we were gratified over the recent decision of the United States Supreme Court," the CIC wrote Earl Brewer, "and we regret that the case must now be tried again in Mississippi."[19] And the NAACP stated that it had hoped that "Mississippi would not retry these men, since the United States Supreme Court in a stinging opinion condemned the torture inflicted upon them and threw out the 'confessions' which were the only evidence against them." "This case," the association added, "is most important, because if won, it will mean a sharp check upon the brutal methods used throughout the South against Negroes."[20]

NAACP secretary Walter White contacted the president of the association's branch in Jackson and pointed out that the national office was, "of course, still interested in the case of Ed Brown, Yank Ellington and Henry Shields." "I hope you and others of the Jackson Branch," White added, "will call on the men from time to time, taking them cigarettes and any other little gifts and letting them know that they have friends during this dark hour."[21]

Since a retrial of the Kemper trio would involve considerable expense, the painful scramble for scarce contributions began again in defense circles, but raising money was even more difficult than before. The NAACP was in a financially desperate condition in the spring of 1936, and the association failed in its attempt to raise money by levying an assessment of a hundred dollars on its Meridian, Mississippi, branch. "I know that the Association is playing a strong part in Brown's, Ellington's and Shields' case in Mississippi," the president of the Meridian branch reported to the NAACP. "We do not want you to feel that we are unmindful of the fact that your organization is doing a great work and, that you are putting more dollars in Mississippi than you are getting out of Mississippi." But, he said, the sum of a hundred dollars was simply beyond the means of the Meridian membership.[22]

The NAACP was finally able to raise forty dollars. This amount was forwarded to the CIC in Atlanta, which added twenty dollars and sent Earl Brewer a check for sixty dollars in early April.[23] In a letter to the CIC in mid-April, Brewer acknowledged this contribution and laid out the status of the case. The "Supreme Court of Mississippi overruled my motion to discharge these boys and remanded their cases back to Kemper County, Mississippi, for retrial," Brewer reported. "I am going to have some expenses in the retrial of this case and since I am contributing a great part of my time and energy to this matter, without cost and without price, I am going to ask if it is possible for your Society along with the N.A.A.C.P. to keep up with the expenses in this trial."[24]

Brewer was apprehensive about the possibility that the Kemper trio would be returned for retrial in Kemper County and might be subjected to a lynch mob. "If these boys are compelled to go back to Kemper County for trial it is going to be necessary for me to get busy and use my influence with the Executive Department of the State to send along military protection for them in that county," Brewer informed the CIC. "With a view of avoiding this, I am going to be compelled to sue out a writ of habeas corpus for them at an early date and undertake to get them discharged and in order to do that I may have to appeal again to the Supreme Court of the United States." "If I fail in this," he continued, "I am going to ask for a change of venue and try and get the case moved out of Kemper County, and whether I fail or succeed in this I am going to ask for a severance so as to give each one of them a separate trial." "In other words," Brewer concluded, "I am going to work on this case and stay with it until I turn these boys loose and I want you people to help me with it, as far as expenses are concerned."[25]

The Commission on Interracial Cooperation responded

to Brewer's appeal for financial aid on 28 April, assuring him that "the Commission . . . will continue to cooperate with you in the defense of Brown, Ellington and Shields." Will Alexander, however, asked that Brewer provide the CIC with "an estimate of the additional amount which will be needed for the expenses in connection with this case."[26] William H. Hewitt, Brewer's associate, replied to the CIC that it was very difficult to estimate what the further expenses in the case would be "due to the fact that we are uncertain just what steps will have to be taken." "However, we plan to file a petition for [a] writ of habeas corpus within the next few weeks, for which proceeding we will probably need about $200.00," Hewitt said. "Of course, if we are unsuccessful in this undertaking, we will make application for a change of venue, for severances, etc., the presentation of which will naturally entail some expense. Naturally, we hope that the matter will be consummated without the necessity of further appeals to higher courts."[27]

In early May, Walter White of the NAACP and Will Alexander discussed the case of the Kemper trio, and both agreed that each of their organizations would endeavor to send a hundred dollars to Earl Brewer as soon as possible.[28] The NAACP was nevertheless still in serious financial trouble, and the top officers of the organization worked without pay the second half of April. Roy Wilkins pointed the situation out to Walter White on 2 May, and informed White that he had "written Lewis Strauss [a contributor to the NAACP] about the Brown, Ellington and Shields case, suggesting he might want to contribute two hundred dollars to it. That will help a little, though at least one hundred dollars of it must be sent to Mississippi without delay."[29]

In some way, the NAACP was able to raise one hundred dollars, and the CIC matched this amount and forwarded two hundred dollars to Earl Brewer on 16 May. "We are glad to be able to assist," the CIC informed Brewer, "in the fine work which you are doing in connection with the Brown, Ellington, and Shields case."[30] Acknowledging his receipt of the money, Brewer said that the contribution "arms me with sufficient power to see what I can do about releasing these boys."[31]

Brewer delayed any further action in the case, however, apparently waiting to see what moves District Attorney John Stennis would make, but the summer of 1936 passed without any new developments in the *Brown* litigation. Brown, Shields, and Ellington remained in the Hinds County jail in Jackson under an order issued by the Sixteenth District Circuit Court requiring Hinds County sheriff John W. Roberts, Jr., to "retain them as at present in jail in your county, pending further developments and also pending further instructions."[32]

Finally, on 5 September, Earl Brewer filed a petition for a writ of habeas corpus in the Hinds County chancery court, seeking the immediate release from custody of the Kemper trio. Brown, Shields, and Ellington were being unlawfully held in the Jackson jail, Brewer argued, because the only evidence that they were guilty of murder had been their confessions, and the U.S. Supreme Court had held those confessions to have been illegally coerced in violation of the Due Process Clause of the Fourteenth Amendment. The petition for a writ of habeas corpus was being filed in Hinds County, rather than in Kemper County, Brewer said, because "the people of Kemper County have been misled and resent . . . [the fact that the *Brown* case was] carried . . . to the United States Supreme Court," with the result that "there seems to be a quiet determination among some of the people in Kemper county to mob the three negroes."[33]

Chancellor V. J. Stricker of the Hinds County chancery court issued the writ of habeas corpus, and ordered that a hearing be held on 10 September before Judge Andrew H. Longino of the Hinds County court to determine whether the Kemper trio should be discharged from custody.[34] Earl Brewer could not have secured a more favorable judge for the hearing, since Andrew Longino was the former governor of the state who had appointed Brewer district attorney of the Eleventh District in 1902.[35] The habeas corpus hearing before Judge Longino was postponed at the request of District Attorney John Stennis, but it was finally held on 19 September, at which time Earl Brewer renewed his contention that the coerced confessions were the only evidence that the Kemper trio had committed any crime, and they therefore were being held unlawfully and should be released from custody. Judge Long-ino agreed with Brewer's argument and therefore ordered Brown, Shields, and Ellington released from the Hinds County jail.[36]

Stennis and the state, however, immediately appealed Longino's decision to Chief Justice Sydney Smith of the Mississippi Supreme Court, and the chief justice reversed the decision to release the Kemper trio. The decision of the U.S. Supreme Court in *Brown* v. *Mississippi*, Smith said, had merely reversed the decision of the state supreme court affirming the convictions of Brown, Shields, and Ellington. The Mississippi Supreme Court, pursuant to the mandate of the U.S. Supreme Court, he pointed out, had entered an order reversing the convictions, but these actions did not affect the validity of the indictment under which the trio were being held. Brown, Shields, and Ellington were therefore not entitled to be released, the chief justice concluded, but should remain in custody pending the disposition of their case by the Circuit Court for the Sixteenth Judicial District, in Kemper County.[37]

During the hearing before Chief Justice Smith, John Stennis and Earl Brewer revealed that they had mutually agreed upon a change of venue if the case were retried, since there was a clear danger of mob action against the defendants in Kemper County.[38] The retrial of the case was finally scheduled for late November at the city of Columbus, in Loundes County. After having spent almost two years in the Hinds County jail in Jackson, the Kemper trio were transferred by Loundes County deputies to the jail in Columbus in late October.[39]

The NAACP and the CIC, in the meantime, were able to raise another $75, and this sum was sent to Earl Brewer on 23 October to help pay for the cost of the retrial.[40] Acknowledging that he had received the money on 26 October, Brewer pointed out to the CIC that he had succeeded "in getting the venue of this case changed out of Kemper County and carried to Loundes County, Mississippi, for trial in the city of Columbus." "I have just returned from a three day trip up there for a conference with the defendants themselves and for the purpose of setting the stage for this trial to take place beginning on the 30th day of November," he continued. "My expenses throughout the habeas corpus [hearing] which I had gone through in this case and obtaining my change of venue, etc., amounted to $12.79 more than the $75.00 check, so I asked Roy Wilkins in a letter today to get busy and help me some before the 30th day of next month. In fact, I expect to leave home three or four days before that date and try to get onto the ground and prepare for this trial."[41]

As the date for the retrial approached, however, District Attorney Stennis contacted Brewer and proposed a plea bargain by which Brown, Shields, and Ellington could plead guilty and receive life imprisonment. Brewer flatly rejected this proposal, but the bargaining between him and Stennis continued. Stennis finally offered to permit the Kemper trio to plead *nolo contendere* to a charge of manslaughter, with the result that Ed Brown would be sentenced to ten years in prison, Henry Shields to five years, and Yank Ellington to three years. With the time the trio had already spent in jail and their good behavior counting against the sentences, however, the sentences would in reality be seven and one-half years for Brown, two and one-half years for Shields, and six months for Ellington.

Ed Brown and Henry Shields were apparently convinced, probably correctly, that no matter how thin the evidence against them might be, a Mississippi jury would convict them, and they would again face a death sentence. When advised by Earl Brewer of the proposed plea bargain, Brown and Shields therefore accepted it. Brewer apparently urged Yank Ellington, on the other hand, not to accept the plea bargain, since there was absolutely no evidence by which he could be convicted on retrial. Ellington, however, said that he preferred to take the six months' sentence because he needed the time to arrange to leave the state safely, being fearful that mob action might yet be taken against him unless he carefully arranged his departure from jail. On 28 November 1936, with the Kemper trio all accepting the plea bargain, the hard-fought battle on their behalf came, rather unsatisfactorily, to an end.[42]

In reporting the plea bargain the Kemper County trio had agreed to, the Jackson *Daily Clarion-Ledger* pointed out that Brown, Shields, and Ellington "have stood within the grim shadow of the hangman's scaffold several times since the dark and dreary . . . night in March 1934 that Raymond [Stuart] was bludgeoned to his death."[43] Editorially, the *Clarion-Ledger* also expressed some dissatisfaction with the way in which the case had ended. "A 'compromise' ends the notorious and costly 'Kemper county' case which gave Mississippi so much undesirable national notoriety," the newspaper said. Pointing out the sentences that Brown, Shields, and Ellington would serve and describing the plea bargain, the *Clarion-Ledger* noted that the result "may seem illogical to many citizens who are not lawyers. The three negroes either were guilty of a murder deserving the death sentence, or they were innocent of all crime." "In the former case, these sentences are ridiculous," the newspaper declared. "In the latter, the sentences are unjust. Many plain citizens will think it would be better for the state's repute either to have forced the three to trial again on the murder indictments, or to have released them. Many will think this despite the fact that the confessions were the only evidence against the three and that, in light of the U.S. Supreme Court decision, the confessions would have been inadmissible in a new trial."[44]

"Despite this, however, the closing of this case is welcomed by all citizens who realize the harm it has done to date," the *Clarion-Ledger* continued. "It is closed, but its lesson should be long remembered by all Mississippi law officers and prosecutors. The lesson is that the use of torture or coercion to obtain confessions not only violates the rights of the accused persons but also jeopardizes Justice. For when confessions thus obtained are thrown out by the trial courts, or the convictions based on them are reversed on appeal, it becomes harder, if not impossible, to obtain a conviction at a second trial, at which the state is handicapped from the start."[45]

Just as the *Clarion-Ledger* was dissatisfied with the way in which the case of the Kemper trio ended, so were those who had been active in organizing the defense of Brown, Shields and Ellington. "It was hoped that the state would not attempt to try the cases again after such a stinging rebuke by the [U.S. Supreme] Court," the NAACP said, "but during several legal delays the state busied itself collecting so-called new evidence, particularly against Ed Brown." John Stennis had revised his offer of a plea bargain several times "until it got down to the sentences finally accepted," the association added. "No move was made to accept the sentences until the defendants themselves were consulted."[46]

As Roy Wilkins said later, the conclusion of the case of the Kemper trio only served to confirm in the NAACP's eyes the prevailing system of injustice imposed upon blacks in the South. "As far as Mississippi was concerned, liberal justice had been meted out," Wilkins observed. "The three field hands were innocent, of course, but then, they hadn't been lynched or electrocuted, had they? To the Magnolia State, jail terms seemed a small price to exact in return for upholding the honor of Mississippi courts against a meddling Supreme Court in Washington. That was the way things were done down South."[47]

Despite the association's disappointment with the way in which *Brown* v. *Mississippi* ended, it was still convinced that it had won a significant victory with the Supreme Court's decision in the case. Writing privately, NAACP secretary Walter White declared that "we are not here to get Negroes out of jail simply because they are Negroes. When we fought for the three sharecroppers in Mississippi—Brown, Ellington and Shields—. . . we were fighting not only for them but for all the millions of helpless, penniless, exploited black sharecroppers—and white ones too—who are in such a desperate plight today." And the U.S. Supreme Court's decision in *Brown* v. *Mississippi*, White added, "in holding that convictions based wholly upon confessions extorted by the third degree. . . [cannot stand], protects, as do most of the Association's activities, the fundamental citizenship rights of white people as well as Negroes. We thus conceive our efforts to be for the wisest interest of America as well as for the specific individuals and cause for which we work."[48]

The case of the Kemper County trio was nevertheless a tragedy for Ed Brown, Henry Shields, and Yank Ellington and their families, of course, and for John A. Clark and his wife as well. Because he alone among the lawyers appointed to defend the trio at their trial had had the courage to take an appeal,

John Clark had seen his political future destroyed as he was defeated for reelection to the state senate in the summer of 1935. And after the first appeal to the Mississippi Supreme Court, Clark's health broke under the strain of the case, and he suffered a physical and mental collapse from which he apparently never recovered. By 1938, Clark had become inactive in the practice of law and his retirement from public life became permanent.[49]

Clark's wife, Matilda Floyd Tann Clark, on the other hand, ran for a seat in the Mississippi house of representatives from Kemper County and was elected in 1939.[50] John Clark accompanied his wife when she traveled to Jackson for the 1940 legislative session, and it was there he died on 25 February at the age of fifty-six. The obituaries published at his death did not mention Clark's role in saving Brown, Shields, and Ellington from the gallows.[51]

Matilda Clark remained active in Mississippi Democratic politics, and she refused to support the Dixiecrat revolt in Mississippi in 1948 against the Truman administration's civil rights program. As a consequence, Mrs. Clark once again was named by the national party as the Democratic national committee woman from Mississippi in 1950, and in 1952 she again challenged the leadership of the Mississippi Democratic party by leading a rival delegation of loyalist Democrats to the national convention. This loyalist delegation was not seated at the convention, however, and after 1952 Mrs. Clark became politically inactive and lived much of the time with a sister in California.[52]

Mrs. Clark died in Jackson on 13 November 1956 at the age of seventy-one.[53] "Many Mississippi women, in addition to her many personal friends, regret and have good reason to regret Mrs. John A. Clark's death at the age of 71 years," the Jackson *Daily Clarion-Ledger* said editorially. She had been, the newspaper said, "an outstanding woman leader, an advocate and worker for women's advance in politics, business and professions," and her "career, standing and services inspired and encouraged many other Mississippi women to seek public offices and to venture into business and professional careers." "Many will long remember her personally," the *Clarion-*

Ledger concluded, "and many other Mississippi women regret her death as a real loss to the state and a serious loss to movements and causes cherished and championed by Mississippi women."[54]

Although Judges William Dozier Anderson and Virgil Alexis Griffith had played important roles in the *Brown* case with their dissents in the Mississippi Supreme Court, there was no political retaliation against them as there had been against John Clark. Judge Anderson, who was the first to call attention to the plight of the Kemper trio by dissenting in the first appeal of the case, continued to serve as a judge on the Mississippi Supreme Court until his retirement in January 1945 at the age of eighty-two.[55] Judge Anderson died on 6 January 1952,[56] and he was praised in the press as having "honored and adhered consistently to the highest ethics of bar and bench throughout his long career, thereby serving well and with distinction his profession, his State, and all people who live under protection of the law."[57]

Judge Griffith's eloquent dissent in the second appeal of the *Brown* case had of course brought national attention to the proceedings involving the Kemper trio, and in 1948 Griffith became chief justice of the Mississippi Supreme Court after the death of Chief Justice Sydney Smith.[58] Griffith served as chief justice only briefly, however, since he retired from the bench on 1 January 1949, at the age of seventy-five.[59] When he died four years later, on 6 October 1953, Chief Justice McGehee of the Mississippi Supreme Court declared that "no judge has served our state in the last 20 years who had a keener legal mind, or a more thorough knowledge of the law, or contributed more to legal jurisprudence in his day than did Judge Griffith."[60]

District Attorney John C. Stennis's political career was also not damaged by the case of the Kemper trio. Indeed, he ultimately became one of the most successful politicans in the history of Mississippi. Judge J. I. Sturdivant, who presided at the trial of Brown, Shields, and Ellington, retired from the bench soon after the trial, resuming the practice of law in Columbus, where he died in the summer of 1939.[61] Sturdivant was replaced on the Circuit Court for the Sixteenth Judicial

District by Judge W. W. Magruder, but Magruder died in February 1937. Governor Hugh White then appointed John Stennis to fill out the remainder of Magruder's term, and Stennis became one of the youngest judges in the state. Stennis had been his choice for the judgeship, Governor White said, because of his "wonderful record as district attorney."[62]

Stennis was elected to a full term on the circuit court in 1938, where he served until 1947. He then became one of five candidates in the Democratic primary seeking to succeed U.S. Senator Theodore Bilbo, who had died in that year. In contrast to the previous demagoguery of Bilbo and some of the other primary candidates, Stennis refused to resort to race baiting in the campaign. "I asked my father what I should say about the race problem," Stennis said. "He told me, 'nothing'—and that is what I am doing in the campaign." Stennis was strongly supported in the primary by Mississippi liberals and by the state's blacks, who called him an "old-fashioned Southern gentleman."[63]

John Stennis won the Democratic primary, a victory that of course assured his election to the U.S. Senate in November 1947, and upon his election, he was praised editorially by the *New York Times*. Stennis, the *Times* said, "has proved his ability and integrity in long service to the state." "The result of the election has a significance beyond the borders of the state," the *Times* declared. "It means that bias, prejudice and hatred are no longer sound campaign currency where they were once so potent. Mississippi has chosen to restore her self-respect through a new Senator she can justly honor."[64] And Stennis went on to become one of the most powerful members of the Senate, where (in 1985) he still serves.

It had been ex-governor Earl Leroy Brewer, however, who, devoting his services to the Kemper trio without fee, had won *Brown* v. *Mississippi* in the U.S. Supreme Court and saved Brown, Shields, and Ellington from the gallows. Brewer continued to practice law in Jackson after the settlement of the *Brown* case, which turned out to be the most spectacular case of his career. Ill health forced him to relinquish his legal practice in the spring of 1941, and he donated his law books to the Hinds County law library. Brewer spent two months in the summer of 1941 resting at his sister's plantation home near Belzoni, but after Christmas of that year he became bedridden.[65]

Earl Brewer died in Jackson on 10 March 1942, and his body lay in state at the Mississippi capitol before he was buried in Clarksdale. Thousands of "Mississippians and others from over the South, where he was widely known," paid tribute to Brewer at his funeral, the press reported. "He died at the age of 74, after a long and useful career," the Jackson *Daily Clarion-Ledger* said of Brewer editorially, "and in his death Mississippi loses another distinguished and useful citizen who gave of his talents to his state."[66] And, it might have been added, he had also unselfishly given his talents to the battle on behalf of the Kemper County trio, and in the process established in *Brown* v. *Mississippi* a principle of permanent significance under the Constitution.

Indeed, largely as a result of Earl Brewer's battle on their behalf, all of the Kemper trio were once again free men by the time of his death in 1942. Having received only a six-month sentence as a result of the plea bargain between John Stennis and Brewer, Yank Ellington actually served approximately five months in prison before he was released on 28 May 1937. Henry Shields was discharged from prison on 6 February 1939, after serving a term of two years and two months. And after being incarcerated just over five years, Ed Brown was discharged from prison on 18 December 1941, four months before Earl Brewer's death.[67]

Although the press had taken pains to point to the decision in *Brown* v. *Mississippi* as vindicating the value of the Supreme Court in the American governmental system, the Court continued to invalidate New Deal legislation throughout 1936. After being overwhelmingly reelected in the fall, President Roosevelt decided that the Court had to be removed as a roadblock to the successful implementation of his program, and one year after the *Brown* decision, Roosevelt announced the plan by which he sought to add six additional justices to the Court. The president thus launched the most serious attack on the Court since the Civil War, and from February 1937 until the following summer, his plan became the center of an acrimonious debate in the Congress and the country at large.

The issue of Roosevelt's court-packing plan, for example, was heatedly debated at the convention of the Mississippi State Bar Association in 1937, and a resolution endorsing the plan was adopted by the convention. Earl Brewer was primarily responsible for pushing the resolution of approval through the convention, and he declared that the court-packing issue pitted the "Mills, the Hoovers, Wall Street, and predatory wealth" against the "white plume of the President."[68]

Despite such support, the court-packing plan was ultimately defeated in the Congress. However, in the face of Roosevelt's proposal, the Supreme Court began in the spring of 1937 to sustain New Deal legislation and to reverse itself with respect to many important constitutional doctrines. Minimum wages had been invalidated by the Court in 1936 as violating liberty of contract and the Due Process Clause, but the Court upheld minimum-wage legislation in the spring of 1937.[69] We know now that the decision to sustain minimum wages was not a product of the court-packing threat,[70] but other decisions of the Court upholding the National Labor Relations Act and the Social Security Act appear to have been clear reversals of the Court's previous attitudes induced by the president's plan.[71] Both Chief Justice Hughes and Justice Roberts had shifted their views on some important issues of constitutional doctrine in the spring of 1937, and began to join the liberal bloc of Brandeis, Cardozo, and Stone to form a majority favorable to New Deal policies. Roosevelt thus lost the battle over the court-packing plan, but he won the war with the Court over the constitutional validity of the New Deal.[72]

After the constitutional crisis of 1937, the Supreme Court abandoned its previous role as censor of socioeconomic policy, leaving such policy to be determined by the elected branches of the government by reversing the constitutional doctrines upon which its role as censor had been based. However, the Court did not abandon the line of development under the Due Process Clause of the Fourteenth Amendment that by the early 1930s pointed toward greater protection of civil liberties under the Fourteenth Amendment—a line of development in which *Brown* v. *Mississippi* became an important point.

This new departure under the Due Process Clause involved both a willingness on the part of the Court to read the liberties of the First Amendment of the Bill of Rights into the Fourteenth Amendment, and an additional trend in the Court's decisions toward tightening the procedural requirements applicable to state criminal proceedings under the Due Process Clause. And both of these lines of development were continued by the Court after 1937, as evidenced by the fact that by 1947, all of the rights guaranteed by the First Amendment of the Bill of Rights had been read into the Due Process Clause by the Court and had thus been made applicable to the states.[73]

In the field of criminal procedure, the Court continued to operate under the fair-trial rule—a rule that required the states under the Due Process Clause to accord criminal defendants fair trials in fact. And under the fair-trial rule, the Court, proceeding in part under the theory of *Twining* v. *New Jersey,*[74] held that a fair trial required the states to recognize some procedural rights similar to rights guaranteed in the Bill of Rights as well as to abstain from certain practices which were nowhere condemned in the Bill of Rights but which nonetheless the Court considered to be incompatible with a fair trial.

In *Moore* v. *Dempsey,*[75] *Tumey* v. *Ohio*[76] and *Mooney* v. *Holohan,*[77] the Court held that a fair trial under the Due Process Clause was denied if the states permitted mob-dominated trials, trials conducted by biased judges, or convictions based on knowingly perjured testimony. In *Powell* v. *Alabama,* on the other hand, the Court ruled that the failure of the states to appoint counsel for indigent defendants in capital and some noncapital cases denied such defendants the right to a fair trial, holding that the Due Process Clause protected a right to counsel similar but not identical to the Sixth Amendment's guarantee of the right to counsel.[78] Similarly, in *Brown* v. *Mississippi* the Court ruled that the use by the states of coerced confessions against defendants, a form of compulsory self-incrimination, also denied the right to a fair trial, with the result that after the *Brown* case the Due Process Clause protected a right similar to the Fifth Amendment's Self-Incrimination Clause.[79]

It is important to note that in *Brown* v. *Mississippi* the Court did not reverse *Twining* v. *New Jersey* nor did it hold that the Self-Incrimination Clause of the Fifth Amendment applied to the states via the Due Process Clause. Rather, as Chief Justice Hughes pointed out in his opinion for the Court in *Brown,* the use of a coerced confession to convict a defendant in a state criminal trial violated the essentials of a fair trial. A trial, Hughes said, was "a mere pretense where the state authorities have contrived a conviction resting solely upon confessions obtained by violence." The use by a state of a confession obtained by physical brutality to convict a defendant, he said, constituted "a wrong so fundamental that it made the whole proceeding a mere pretense of a trial and rendered the conviction and sentence wholly void."[80] The *Brown* decision was thus an extension of the fair-trial rule that had emerged in the *Moore–Tumey–Mooney–Powell* line of cases, and coerced confessions were condemned by the Court, not because the Self-Incrimination Clause of the Fifth Amendment applied to the states, but because the use of coerced confessions by the states to convict criminal defendants violated the essentials of a fair trial as mandated by the Due Process Clause.

Brown v. *Mississippi* nevertheless was the first case in which the Supreme Court reversed a state criminal conviction on the ground of coerced confessions, and the case opened the door to a long line of decisions by the Court in which state convictions were reversed because coerced confessions had been used to convict defendants. As the number of coerced-confession cases burgeoned after 1936, the Court formulated the "totality-of-the-circumstances" rule, used to determine whether a confession had been coerced, in which case its use as evidence in a state trial was condemned by the Due Process Clause. Under this rule, the Court would examine all of the circumstances under which a confession had been elicited to determine whether it had been the product of coercion, proceeding on a case-by-case basis.[81] And although it had condemned in the *Brown* case the use of confessions obtained by especially barbarous methods of physical brutality, the Court soon came to recognize that confessions could be coerced through psychological methods as well.[82]

In the 1940s and '50s, therefore, the totality-of-the-circumstances rule, as interpreted in the decisions of the Court, came to impose progressively more restrictive standards upon the states under the Due Process Clause, standards that came to closely resemble the Self-Incrimination Clause of the Fifth Amendment. Justice Felix Frankfurter declared in 1961 that coerced confessions were excluded under the Due Process Clause "not because such confessions are unlikely to be true but because the methods used to extract them offend an underlying principle in the enforcement of our criminal law; that ours is an accusatorial and not an inquisitorial system—a system in which the State must establish guilt by evidence independently and freely secured and may not by coercion prove its charge against an accused out of his own mouth."[83]

Despite the fact that it was formulating progressively stricter standards governing coerced confessions in state cases, in the 1960s the Court came to be dominated by a majority of justices who supported the "selective incorporation" of the Bill of Rights under the Due Process Clause of the Fourteenth Amendment. The selective incorporationists believed that most of the rights in the Bill of Rights should be applied to the states via the Due Process Clause, and when a right from the Bill of Rights so applied, it should apply in an identical way to the states as it applied to the federal government. The selective incorporationists therefore rejected the 1923 fair-trial rule of *Moore* v. *Dempsey* —that the Due Process Clause guaranteed rights similar but not identical to some of the rights in the Bill of Rights.[84]

A majority of the Court thus abandoned the fair-trial rule in the 1960s and began to "incorporate" most of the criminal-procedure provisions of the Bill of Rights into the Due Process Clause of the Fourteenth Amendment, making those provisions apply to the states in the identical way in which they applied to the federal government. In 1963, for example, the Court held in *Gideon* v. *Wainwright* that the Assistance of Counsel Clause of the Sixth Amendment applied to the states via the Due Process Clause in the identical way in which it had always applied in federal criminal proceedings.[85] As a result of the *Gideon* ruling, indigent defendants were henceforth entitled to an absolute right to appointed counsel in all serious state criminal proceedings,[86] and the question was no longer whether the absence of counsel would result in an unfair trial, as had been the test under *Powell* v. *Alabama* and the cases that had followed in its wake.[87]

In the following year, the Court reversed *Twining* v. *New Jersey* and held in *Malloy* v. *Hogan* that the Self-Incrimination Clause of the Fifth Amendment applied to the states via the Due Process Clause, again ruling that the Self-Incrimination Clause applied to the states in the identical way in which it applied to federal proceedings. The fair-trial rule, that the Due Process Clause guaranteed a right only similar to the Self-Incrimination Clause as recognized in *Brown* v. *Mississippi*, was thus abandoned by the Court.[88]

With the Assistance of Counsel Clause of the Sixth Amendment and the Self-Incrimination Clause of the Fifth Amendment being fully applicable to the states by the mid-1960s, the Court next turned to a reevaluation of its approach to the issue of coerced confessions. And in *Miranda* v. *Arizona*, the Court abandoned the totality-of-the-circumstances rule that had emerged after the *Brown* decision, holding instead that when an individual was in custody and a police investigation had come to focus upon that individual as the principal suspect in a crime, any interrogation for the purpose of eliciting a confession must be preceded by a warning advising the suspect of the right to silence under the Self-Incrimination Clause and the right to counsel under the Sixth Amendment. "The defendant may waive effectuation of these rights, provided the waiver is made voluntarily, knowingly and intelligently," Chief Justice Warren said in the *Miranda* opinion. "If, however, he indicates in any manner and at any stage of the process that he wishes to consult with an attorney before speaking there can be no questioning. Likewise, if the individual is alone and indicates in any manner that he does not wish to be interrogated, the police may not question him."[89]

The Supreme Court announced its decision in *Miranda* v. *Arizona* in June 1966. Thirty-two years previously, Ed Brown,

Henry Shields, and Yank Ellington had sat in the county jail in Meridian, recovering from wounds inflicted to secure their confessions to the murder of Raymond Stuart. The litigation in their case had begun the process of constitutional development that had culminated in the *Miranda* decision—a decision imposing standards of constitutional conduct upon law enforcement agencies that seems light years, rather than just over thirty years, away from the treatment of the Kemper County trio in 1934.

1. *New York Times*, 21 Feb. 1936, p. 16, editorial, "What the Court 'Obstructs'."

2. Washington *Post*, 19 Feb. 1936, p. 8, editorial, "A Stroke for Human Rights."

3. Chicago *Tribune*, 15 March 1936, pt. 7, p. 5. There were, however, inaccuracies in the *Tribune's* coverage of the *Brown* case. District Attorney John C. Stennis was identified as "John B. Stennis"; the account listed only John A. Clark and "B. T. Davis" as defense counsel at the trial, while there had of course been four such attorneys; the *Tribune* asserted that neither Davis nor Clark "took part in the subsequent appeal of the case," although Clark had taken the first appeal to the Mississippi Supreme Court and had therefore played a significant role in saving the Kemper trio from the gallows; and the *Tribune* generally characterized Earl Brewer inaccurately, asserting that he had "spent a fortune in fighting legal battles for unfortunates unable to finance a defense or an appeal," while there is no evidence that Brewer had engaged in such activities.

4. St. Louis *Post Dispatch*, 18 Feb. 1936, p. 26, editorial, "Human Rights Upheld." Editorial comments favorable to the Court's decision were also published in the New York *Daily Mirror*, New York *World-Telegram*, New York *Post*, San Antonio *Evening News*, and Philadelphia *Tribune*. See NAACP Press Release, 21 Feb. 1936, CIC Papers; *Crisis* 43 (April 1936): 115.

5. *Chicago Defender*, 29 Feb. 1936, p. 16, editorial, "Supreme Court Reverses Mississippi Mock Trial."

6. *Nation* 142 (4 March 1936): 263–64.

7. There were, for example, no editorial comments in such leading Southern newspapers as the New Orleans *Times-Picayune*, Arkansas *Gazette*, or Atlanta *Constitution*.

8. Chattanooga *Daily Times*, 19 Feb. 1936, p . 6, editorial, "The Mississippi Case."

9. Memphis *Commercial Appeal,* 19 Feb. 1936, p. 6, editorial, "Baiting the Supreme Court."

10. Jackson *Daily News,* 19 Feb. 1936, p. 6, editorial, "One United States Supreme Court Decision."

11. Jackson *Daily Clarion-Ledger,* 20 Feb. 1936, p. 6, editorial, "Supreme Court Decision Right But Gives Us Costly Publicity."

12. Jackson *Daily News,* 18 Feb. 1936, p. 13.

13. Ibid.

14. Memorandum for Mr. Wilkins for the Board Report, 3 March 1936, NAACP Papers, D–12.

15. Digest of Outstanding Cases Handled by the NAACP during 1935, 14 April 1936, NAACP Papers, D–12.

16. *Chicago Defender,* 22 Feb. 1936, p. 1.

17. Jackson *Daily News,* 13 April 1936, p. 1.

18. Meridian *Star,* 24 Feb. 1936, p. 1.

19. Emily H. Clay to Earl Brewer, 7 April 1936, CIC Papers.

20. Digest of Outstanding Cases Handled by the NAACP during 1935, 14 April 1936, NAACP Papers, D–12.

21. Walter White to A. W. Wells, 25 March 1936, ibid., G–105.

22. R. L. Young to Mary White Ovington, 1 April 1936, ibid., G–106.

23. Roy Wilkins to Will Alexander, 4 April 1936; Emily H. Clay to Earl Brewer, 7 April 1936, CIC Papers.

24. Earl Brewer to CIC, 16 April 1936, ibid.

25. Ibid.

26. Emily H. Clay to Earl Brewer, 20 April 1936, ibid.

27. W. H. Hewitt to Emily H. Clay, 5 May 1936, ibid.

28. Emily H. Clay to Earl Brewer, 13 May 1936, ibid.

29. Roy Wilkins to Walter White, 2 May 1936, NAACP Papers, C–80.

30. Emily H. Clay to Earl Brewer, 16 May 1936, CIC Papers.

31. Earl Brewer to Emily H. Clay, 18 May 1936, ibid.

32. Jackson *Daily Clarion-Ledger,* 6 Sept. 1936, p. 12; the order was dated 12 March 1936.

33. Ibid.

34. Ibid.

35. Martha Harrison Williford and Claudia Brewer Strite, "Biography of Earl Leroy Brewer" (unpublished ms.), p. 8.

36. Jackson *Daily Clarion-Ledger,* 20 Sept. 1936, pp. 1, 12.

37. Ibid.

38. Ibid.

39. Ibid., 21 Oct. 1936, p. 2.

40. Emily H. Clay to Earl Brewer, 23 Oct. 1936; Roy Wilkins to CIC, 21 Oct. 1936, CIC Papers.

41. Earl Brewer to CIC, 26 Oct. 1936, ibid.

42. NAACP Press Service, News Release, 11 Dec. 1936, ACLU Archives, vol. 919; Jackson *Daily Clarion-Ledger,* 29 Nov. 1936, p. 1; Meridian *Star,* 29 Nov. 1936, p. 1.

43. Jackson *Daily Clarion-Ledger,* 29 Nov. 1936, p. 1.

44. Ibid., 1 Dec. 1936, p. 6, editorial, "A Somewhat Strange Compromise Closes the 'Kemper County Case'."

45. Ibid.

46. NAACP Press Service, News Release, 11 Dec. 1936, ACLU Archives, vol. 919.

47. Roy Wilkins, *Standing Fast: The Autobiography of Roy Wilkins* (New York: Viking Press, 1982), p. 167.

48. Walter White to Bill Robinson, 11 Dec. 1936, NAACP Papers, C–156.

49. Clark had become an inactive member of the Mississippi Bar Association in 1938; see *Mississippi Law Journal* 10 (1938): 511, (1938–39): 597.

50. Meridian *Star,* 9 Aug. 1939, p. 5; 10 Aug. 1939, p. 10; 10 Sept. 1939, p. 6; Jackson *Daily Clarion-Ledger,* 24 Jan. 1940, p. 14.

51. Jackson *Daily Clarion-Ledger,* 26 Feb. 1940, p. 1; Meridian *Star,* 26 Feb. 1940, p. 3.

52. James H. McLendon, *Democratic Presidential Politics in Mississippi in 1952* (State College: Mississippi State College Social Science Studies, Government Series No. 9, Sept. 1953), pp. 7–15. Jackson *Daily Clarion-Ledger,* 20 July 1952, p. 5; 16 July 1956, p. 11; *New York Times,* 27 June 1952, p. 8; 19 July 1952, p. 7.

53. Jackson *Daily Clarion-Ledger,* 14 Nov. 1956, p. 6; 15 Nov. 1956, p. 4; Meridian *Star,* 14 Nov. 1956, p. 18. Mrs. Clark's age at her death was variously reported as seventy and seventy-one.

54. Jackson *Daily Clarion-Ledger,* 17 Nov. 1956, p. 6, editorial, "Our Women Lose a Noted Leader."

55. Ibid., 9 Jan. 1945, p. 10.

56. Ibid., 7 Jan. 1952, p. 1.

57. Ibid., 8 Jan. 1952, p. 4, editorial, "William Dozier Anderson: Eminent Jurist and Citizen."

58. Ibid., 25 July 1948, pp. 1, 12; 30 July 1948, p. 4.

59. Ibid., 1 Jan. 1949, pp. 1, 3; 2 Jan. 1949, p. 1.

60. Ibid., 8 Oct. 1953, p. 16, editorial, "Judge Griffith Made Many Fine Contributions."

61. Meridian *Star,* 20 Nov. 1939, p. 10, reporting memorial resolutions presented by the bar in honor of Sturdivant.

62. Jackson *Daily Clarion-Ledger,* 11 Feb. 1937, p. 6; 10 Feb. 1937, p. 16.

63. *New York Times,* 6 Nov. 1947, pp. 21, 26.

64. Ibid., 6 Nov. 1947, p. 26.

65. Williford and Strite, "Biography" p. 24.

66. Jackson *Daily Clarion-Ledger*, 11 March 1942, p. 1; 12 March 1942, p. 1; 12 March 1942, p. 6, editorial, "Gov. Earl Leroy Brewer Is Mourned by Mississippi."

67. Letter from Christine Houston, Director of Records, Mississippi Department of Corrections, to author, 6 July 1984. In his book, *The Petitioners* (New York: Pantheon Books, 1966), p. 280, Loren Miller states that after the decision of the U.S. Supreme Court in the *Brown* case, the Kemper trio "were never retried. They later made what amounted to a farcical 'escape' and were never apprehended." This of course is incorrect, since the prison records demonstrate that the trio served their prison sentences.

68. Martha H. Swain, *Pat Harrison: The New Deal Years* (Jackson: University Press of Mississippi, 1978), p. 149. On the court-packing fight generally, see Joseph Alsop and Turner Catledge, *The 168 Days* (Garden City, N.Y.: Doubleday, Doran, 1938), and Leonard Baker, *Back to Back: The Duel between FDR and the Supreme Court* (New York: Macmillan, 1967).

69. West Coast Hotel v. Parrish, 300 U.S. 379 (1937), reversing Morehead v. New York, 298 U.S. 587 (1936).

70. See Richard C. Cortner, *The Wagner Act Cases* (Knoxville: University of Tennessee Press, 1964), pp. 170–71.

71. Ibid., pp. 176–77.

72. Ibid., pp. 177–78.

73. See Richard C. Cortner, *The Supreme Court and the Second Bill of Rights* (Madison: University of Wisconsin Press, 1981), pp. 63–123.

74. 211 U.S. 78 (1908). For an analysis of the *Twining* case, see Cortner, *Supreme Court and Second Bill of Rights*. pp. 38–50.

75. 261 U.S. 86 (1923).

76. 273 U.S. 510 (1927).

77. 293 U.S. 103 (1935).

78. 287 U.S. 45 (1932).

79. 297 U.S. 278 (1936).

80. Ibid., p. 286.

81. See David Fellman, *The Defendant's Rights Today* (Madison: University of Wisconsin Press, 1976), p. 41.

82. Ashcraft v. Tennessee, 322 U.S. 143 (1944).

83. Rogers v. Richmond, 365 U.S. 534, 540–41 (1961).

84. For an analysis of the selective-incorporationist position, see Cortner, *Supreme Court and Second Bill of Rights*, pp. 173–76.

85. 372 U.S. 335 (1963).

86. In Argersinger v. Hamlin, 407 U.S. 25 (1972), the Court held that a serious criminal case is one in which loss of liberty is at stake.

87. See Cortner, *Supreme Court and Second Bill of Rights*, pp. 193–204.

88. 378 U.S. 1 (1964).

89. Miranda v. Arizona, 384 U.S. 436, 444–45 (1966). For an analysis of the *Miranda* case, see Richard C. Cortner and Clifford M. Lytle, *Modern Constitutional Law* (New York: Free Press, 1971), pp. 158-98.

A Note On Sources

In documenting the course of the litigation in *Brown* v. *Mississippi*, 297 U.S. 278 (1936), I have relied extensively upon data contained in three manuscript collections: the American Civil Liberties Union (ACLU) Archives, located in the Seeley G. Mudd Library at Princeton University; the Commission on Interracial Cooperation (CIC) papers in the Atlanta University Center–Woodruff Library, at Atlanta, Georgia; and the papers of the National Association for the Advancement of Colored People (NAACP), which have been deposited in the Manuscript Division of the Library of Congress. References to data from the ACLU Archives are identified in the notes by the designation "ACLU Archives," along with the citation of the appropriate volume number. The data on the *Brown* case in the Commission on Interracial Cooperation papers are located in Box 17-B-7-c, Legal Aid, in that collection and are identified here by the designation "CIC Papers." The NAACP Papers in the Library of Congress are filed according to a system with letter and number designations. The NAACP data cited here are identified as "NAACP Papers," followed by the letter and number indicating their location in that collection.

Finally, the briefs and record in *Brown* v. *Mississippi* used in this study are available in the microcard edition of Supreme Court briefs and records produced by Information Handling Services.

Index

CPSIA information can be obtained at www.ICGtesting.com
Printed in the USA
LVOW04s0901010815

448429LV00017B/174/P